AMAZE YOURSELF
Take a Quantum Leap...

I0132521

Soft Cover Edition
September 2014

By
Dr. Jill Ammon-Wexler
http://www.BuildMindPower.com

Dr. Jill Ammon-Wexler

ISBN-13: 978-0991037964 (Quantum Self Group, Inc)
ISBN-10: 0991037960

Soft Cover Edition

Published by
Quantum Self Group, Inc
217 Cedar Street #268
Sandpoint, Idaho 83864 USA

AUTHOR'S INTRODUCTION...

Have you ever wondered why most personal development books and programs often leave you right back where you started?

It's not that there's anything "wrong" with you. It's just that most of these programs and books are based on an old assumption that change must be slow and gradual – the "one-step-at-a-time" method. Does this work? You already know the answer! This method is like trying to strike oil with a pick and shovel.

Assuming you're about to read this book – that's about to change for you! Here's what I have discovered over my four plus decades as a transformational psychologist: No matter how intelligent you are, no matter how creative or successful, there's still more waiting to emerge. Plus no matter how "limited" or "challenged" you might think you are, there is a charismatic, bright and far more capable version of you just waiting for an invitation to emerge.

Just reading this book will trigger personal change. How can this be so? I discovered years ago that certain INSIGHTS alone create instant quantum leaps in one's natural genius, personal charisma, passion, motivation, personal power, and achievement.

What IS a quantum leap? In terms of quantum physics, it is the appearance of a particle at an entirely new location without passing through the space between the stopping and starting location. In effect, it simply INSTANTLY appears in an entirely new state.

There is no "magic" here. This is a very practical, insightful guide to taking a virtual quantum leap into a far more empowered version of YOU.

Dr. Jill Ammon-Wexler

HERE'S WHAT YOU'LL EXPERIENCE...

Immediate **SUPERCHARGED CONFIDENCE.** Learn why it's perfectly OK to be totally "imperfect." This will instantly boost your confidence from the inside-out. The effect of this insight immediately moves you UP to the next level in your life.

Discover YOUR NATURAL GENIUS. Modern science has proven that genius-level creative skills are NOT born, they are learnable. Begin to have actual genius-level "ah-ha" insights, and learn an exciting way to conduct your own personal creative brainstorms.

FEEL GREAT EVERY DAY. Learn and apply the shocking scientific proof (and simple proven techniques) you can use to instantly experience GENUINE HAPPINESS. This amazing technique works immediately, and yields extremely exciting and enjoyable results.

TAKE CHARGE of stress. We live in a high-stress world. Ever feel like your mind was running off without you? Stress is NOT what you think it is. This amazing insight into what stress really is puts YOU in immediate control!

Meet YOUR "HIGHER SELF." There's now strong scientific evidence we ALL have extra-sensory powers. Learn what this is all about, and why many businesses are using the services of people with refined paranormal and psychic powers. Learn the truth about your physical "third eye."

STOP MENTAL AGING. We begin to lose our mental edge after 30, and build Alzheimer's brain tangles long before any memory problems show up. Learn how to build a neural reserve to totally avoid "losing your mind," even if you do get Alzheimer's 5, 10, 20 or 40 years from now. Protect your mind power.

BREAK OUT OF THE BOX. Learn why feelings of restlessness, boredom and feeling stuck are actually a GREAT SIGN! Take steps to prepare to take a quantum leap into a powerful new personal reality.

Learn to ENTER "THE FLOW." There's an old assumption that super-achiever performance is beyond the reach of "ordinary" people. Wrong! Learn why "the Flow" is a natural brain state, and take steps to take to rapidly pop into this remarkable high-performance experience.

TAKE A QUANTUM LEAP. Do you assume it's impossible to create an instant personal change and have it last? You'll blast past that old myth as you are guided step-by-step into a very real personal quantum leap.

Life will NEVER be the same!

Dr. Jill Ammon-Wexler

CONTENTS

1. POWER OF CONFIDENCE........... 13
Not a Born Extrovert?
Are We Born Self-Confident?
Are YOU Confident?
Ever Feel Like "a Fake?"
Why Make a Change?

2. YOUR SELF CONCEPT................. 23
The Power of Emotion
A "Self-Esteem" Strategy

3. THE POWER OF EMOTION 29
"Self-Esteem" Strategy
Learn Genius-Level Creativity
The "Creative Genius" Myth
Increase Your Natural Genius
Sharpen Your Creative Skills
Get More Brilliant Insights
A New "Insights" Strategy
A "Creative Brainstorming" Exercise

4. FEEL GREAT EVERY DAY............ 47
Anger Can Make You Happy
Use Anger Positively
Create Solid Belief
How This Works
Feel Great Now

5. THE BUBBLE MACHINE 61

What Stress Is NOT
Calm the "Monkey Mind"
Embrace Change
Habits and Stress

6. GO BEYOND "ORDINARY" 79

"Paranormal" is Normal
Is Someone Staring at You?
Walking Through Walls?
Successful Executives Do It
Your Odd Third Eye
Stretch Past "Ordinary"
Simple Meditation Experiment
Sound Toning for Mental Clarity

7. TURN BACK THE CLOCK 93

Advantages of Older Brains
What About Alzheimer's?
The Answer is the Brain
What Caused The Difference?
Do We "Think" Ourselves Old?
Get Started Today
Pursue Healthy Longevity

8. WHAT DO YOU WANT? 117

Stuck in a Box?
How Success Happens
Food For Thought

Get "On Purpose"
ACT Like a Winner

9. FLOW INTO HIGHER STATES **137**
"Higher States" Are Attainable
The Secret of Entering "Flow"
What IS the Flow?
Flow Builds Mind Power
Being in "The Flow"
How to Get Started With "The Flow

10. YOUR QUANTUM LEAP **151**
Rapid Change = True Power
Prepare For a Quantum Leap
You CAN Do It!
Quantum Leaps and Physics
How to Move Forward
Life Begins When YOU Do

11. OUR OTHER OFFERINGS **173**
Your Next Step?
Like to Explore?
Brain Training Audios
The Ultimate Goal System
Build a Quantum Mind

MEET THE AUTHOR **177**

Dr. Jill Ammon-Wexler

ONE. THE POWER OF CONFIDENCE

What follows is an amazing true story that could change how you view your own life – only the name has been changed.

Margie Ma's childhood was far less than perfect. From early childhood she collected deep scars from her mother's constant biting criticism, her father's cold indifference, and ongoing painful comparison to her popular older brother.

Margie developed very little self-esteem and even less self-confidence. Early in childhood she began to avoid unnecessary social contact. That habit followed her into adulthood.

At 18 Margie married one of her brother's friends and quietly devoted herself to raising their children --still avoiding social contact whenever possible.

Late one Saturday afternoon on her way to pick up her daughter from ballet class, Margie's sheltered life was suddenly shattered.

She was only two blocks from the ballet studio when a distracted driver plowed into her Ford Focus going an estimated 60 miles an hour.

The accident scene was horrifying. Firemen had to use the "Jaws of Life" to cut Margie out of her mangled car. When they finally pulled her out she was unconscious and hanging onto life by a very, very thin thread.

Margie came out of her coma in the hospital six days later. Her head was bandaged, her neck clamped into a brace, a tube shoved down her throat, her right leg suspended from the ceiling, and a dripping IV was taped to her arm. The irritating beep to her left proved to be a life sign monitor.

The young woman had no idea how she ended up in that hospital room. In fact, her memory was wiped totally clean. She remembered nothing of the accident, her past history, her family, or her name. In short, her entire identify had been wiped from her memory.

Can you imagine her shock and alarm? Once home Margie had to become reacquainted with her children and husband.

She began to read medical texts trying to understand her situation, and even wrote a paper about her experiences. Her doctor invited her to present her paper at local medical meeting and Margie agreed. Her presentation led to an invitation to present it at a state medical convention. Again she agreed.

An interesting thing was happening to Margie.

Since she no longer had a "personal history," her life experiences began to create a personality quite different from her now forgotten self. The positive attention she received was forging a powerful sense of self-esteem and confidence. Interestingly, Margie gradually became an extremely confident, outgoing woman.

Is that amazing? This is the real story of a very real woman. Obviously you don't want a major accident and coma in your life. But here's the point: It's truly possible to create a powerful NEW sense of confidence and high self-esteem from the ground up, regardless of your personal past history.

Not a Born Extrovert?

Is the secret to achieving higher levels of success and happiness being born a natural extrovert?

It does often seem that some people are just naturally born confident, and perhaps they are more extroverted and outgoing as children. But is extroversion necessarily a sign of self confidence?

Others seem to be more naturally introverted even as children. Is this necessarily a sign they have lower self confidence, as is often assumed?

The evidence is NO! This is one of those insights with the potential to immediately change how you view your own potential.

Our behavior is molded from birth by the primary caregivers in our life. A child might have a natural tendency to be outgoing, but that can be snuffed out very quickly by the demands of that child's environment.

If it is not safe to show one's emotions, for example, a child will quickly discover ways to repress them. This alone can change a "born extrovert" into a deeply closed-down introvert.

Are We Born Self-Confident?

Self-confidence is a vital ingredient of happiness. Without it you often won't even try to do or be what you are really capable of.

Regardless of your upbringing, after my four plus decades as a psychologist I can assure you that extroverts are *not* always confident, and introverts do *not* necessarily lack confidence.

Both extroverts and introverts can have unwavering certainty about their own abilities, the most basic sign of self-confidence and healthy self-esteem.

It is important to recognize that no one is necessarily born confident. Self-confidence is <u>built</u> through life experience.

If you have collected a lifetime of negative beliefs about your own abilities, for example, you'll tend have low self-confidence. That is, unless you DO something about it.

Doing something about it starts with the recognition that YOU are in charge. Consider Margie's story. As you read on you will discover some proven-effective ways to immediately change how both you and others view as your level of self-confidence. The secret is to just take a little action.

Are YOU Confident?

Most people agree on the outward signs of self-confidence: The ability to express one's self openly, to try something new, or to take action in spite of what others might say or do.

According to Webster's, confidence is, "Having no uncertainty about one's abilities." This sums it up pretty well. But if you do not believe in yourself and your abilities, that belief becomes your own internal truth and creates the reality of your life.

How do you recognize IF your life is being limited by low self-confidence? You know it because when you feel the desire to try something new, a critical voice rises up from your subconscious mind and stops you cold.

If you are unhappy and not achieving your life goals, there's a high probability the culprit is a lack of confidence. The same is true if you tend to procrastinate, or lack the belief you can improve your life. Whatever you believe to be true about yourself IS the truth for you, BUT THAT CAN CHANGE.

Ever Feel Like "a Fake?"

Other people can praise you and make you feel good. But if you do not truly believe in your self, their praise and recognition may just make you feel like a "fake." Why? Because you feel in your heart you aren't really who or what they are praising and recognizing -- even though *they* can see it!

Here's something you NEED to know: The feeling you're a "fake" may come up when you're actually in the midst of personal growth and are stretching and expanding.

This happens because at the heart of growth is introspection. And as you examine yourself you will always uncover some personal "imperfections." Such personal "imperfections" are just part of being human.

There will always be "something" going on inside that is less than perfect. But you are probably judging yourself unfairly. Maybe it's time to allow yourself to be "perfectly imperfect."

19

Why Make a Change?

The fact is, if you do not believe in yourself and your abilities, that belief *becomes* your internal truth. So a good place to start is by ironing out any kinks in what you believe about your own self.

Here are several things you'll want to know about self-esteem:

- Your self-esteem is at the very CORE of your being. It molds literally everything you believe about yourself.

- Low self-esteem is NOT your fault. It began with a "less than perfect" childhood. True … the past can't be changed. But it is past, after all. And you obviously did survive it!

- Most of what you believe to be your limitations or shortcomings are probably NOT even true for you at all today. They are just habitual ways of thinking. And habits can be changed!

- Low self-esteem does not just "go away." What you believe about yourself is behind your every thought, action, and inaction in your life. It's the source of your procrastination, negative thinking, and lack of motivation -- anything that holds you back.

Any change in your life conditions must begin with a change in how you view yourself. Take a moment to consider how your life would improve if you begin to allow yourself and others to be "perfectly imperfect."

Dr. Jill Ammon-Wexler

TWO. YOUR SELF CONCEPT

No one is born with high self-esteem and confidence, and you're NOT wrong or weak if you feel lacking in these traits! More likely this is just a sign you didn't get the level of support you needed as a child; but that too can be OK now.

Muhammad Ali, an all-time great champion boxer said, "To be a great champion you must believe you are the best. If you're not, *pretend* you are."

Your self-concept is stored deep in your subconscious mind. Why is that important? Our brains naturally look to the past to interpret today's reality. So your brain might endlessly "revisit" old experiences that created feelings of low self-confidence.

Every time a memory recalled in the present, the brain connections holding that memory are physically strengthened.

The Power of Emotion

The secret of getting your brain on your side is emotion! If you tie intense emotion to NEW images of high self confidence, your subconscious mind will accept them as true.

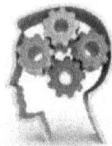

Actually your subconscious mind does NOT know the difference between imagined reality and "real" reality. This is a fact proven by many scientific researchers, and underscores the importance of emotional power.

It is very powerful to surround your goals with emotional desire. This not only builds and sustains your motivation, the importance of that goal will build in your subconscious mind.

The more intense your emotion, the more rapidly you'll notice your life shifting and changing. Add some loving acceptance of yourself to this, and any tendency toward low self-esteem and lack of confidence will begin to take care of itself.

A "Self-Esteem" Strategy

A good personal mission is to discover your own unique personal strengths. We all have them, and YOU are no exception. Avoid the tendency to dwell on your "personal limitations."

Always remember that what you focus on will grow. This is a physical brain reality, so it is far smarter to focus on your strengths rather than your perceived "weaknesses."

Do you feel you have the power to call the shots in your life, or do you feel you have no control over your own destiny?

The answer to this question provides a measure of your self-esteem. How you feel about yourself affects every aspect of your life. When your self-esteem is high, problems are not viewed as threats, but as opportunities for success. High self-esteem puts you in charge of your life.

You do not have to spend years in counseling to become more confident and increase your self-esteem. Studies show that focus on the following can move you forward rapidly.

Your Signature Strengths. We each have our own unique "signature strengths." Take a few minutes to write down your top five strengths. Avoid overlooking something because it seems too "unimportant." It is very easy to assume that because something is easy for you, it is not an important personal strength. Wrong! Get it on your list!

Experimenters had a research group do this, and then use one of their strengths in a new and different way each day for one week.

The results were amazing. The study group had measurable increases in self-esteem and happiness that were still present six months later. Imagine what can happen in your life if you make this a daily habit!

Recognize Your Successes. Another research study had a group of adults write down three things that had gone well that day, and why they felt those things went well. Again, although the experiment lasted only one week, the participants reported still feeling happier six months later.

What if you were to create a habit of doing this at the end of each day? Can you imagine the boost you would get to your self-confidence and self-esteem?

When doing this be sure not to overlook or reject a successful experience by insisting it was too unimportant or does not count for some reason. Give yourself credit for the smallest accomplishments. Success builds success!

Just ACT Confident. One quick way to increase your confidence is to simply ACT confident. Does this seem too simple? This is actually a major insight that can instantly change your life!   Studies of the "act as if" approach prove it has a very strong and immediate impact on confidence and self-esteem.

Scientists at Wake Forest University had 50 students simply "*act* like confident extroverts" for 15 minutes during a group discussion, even if they didn't feel confident. Interestingly, the more assertive and energetic the students acted, the more confident they *actually* became. *Think about this!*

Create Positive Beliefs. When it comes to building self-esteem, it's very helpful to create some positive beliefs about yourself. Start by paying attention to what you say to yourself about you. Negative self-talk creates negative internal images. Correct this by paying more attention to the things you appreciate about yourself.

THREE. YOUR CREATIVE SPARK

A wild-haired scientist has spent the entire day struggling with an unsolved question. He's frustrated and exhausted. Suddenly he leans back in his chair and opens a small desk drawer.

He pulls out two walnut-sized black stones, places one in each hand and then drapes his arms over the sides of his chair.

You watch as his eyelids flicker and close gently. The tension begins to fall from his body. His forehead, shoulders, and even his neck muscles relax. He slumps slightly in the chair, still holding the small black stones.

Now visualize tiny EEG sensors hooked up to the scientist's forehead. You watch as his brainwaves slide down into the slower range associated with sleep. But that's not what he wants to do. The sound of the small rocks hitting the floor would wake him, should he drift too close to sleep.

You see a tiny spike of Beta (conscious thinking) brainwaves as a string of thoughts slide into his subconscious "thought-stream."

Twenty minutes later he abruptly sits up, drops the rocks on his desk, and grabs a pen. The famed Albert Einstein has just pulled an answer from out of his rich subconscious storehouse.

Albert Einstein
A master of creative thinking

More than one deep thinker down through the ages has been spotted "nodding off" into what looks like a nap – while in fact they were actively entering a very high-creativity brain state.

Learn Genius-Level Creativity

Creativity is often viewed as a characteristic of a few gifted geniuses. There's Picasso in art, Callas in Opera, Henry Ford in manufacturing, Beethoven in classical music, Bill Gates in business, Einstein in science, Leonardo da Vinci in visionary inventing, and so on.

True, probably not everyone can be a Beethoven or Picasso or Einstein; but bright creative ideas are *not* limited to a few geniuses. We each have the capability of natural creative genius built right into our physical brains.

Actually creativity goes far beyond the ability to paint, write, create a new business, fill a great hall with your voice, or invent a new product. You can immediately unleash far more creativity by simply adjusting how you think about the process of creativity itself.

Creativity is at the heart of EVERY action that changes your inner or outer reality.

You are actually being "creative" when you prowl through the refrigerator searching for "sandwich makings."

So ... why then do so few of us consider ourselves creative? Remember when you were seven years old and just starting your formal education? There you were, full of raw unbridled creativity and enthusiasm.

Then what was the first thing that happened? You were told to sit still in an uncomfortable little desk, be quiet, and raise your hand for permission to even speak. Does that sound like a creative environment?

Unfortunately, most formal education systems put emphasis on conformity, order and control. Small wonder many have a tough time being spontaneous and creative as adults.

The "Creative Genius" Myth

Many, many people have been intimidated by the "natural creative genius myth" -- the assumption that true creativity is limited to a few natural born creative geniuses. That myth was actually shot down years ago.

Back in the 1920's a group of California teachers selected 1,528 school children with a "genius-level IQ" for a long-term study. A series of research teams then followed these children over 60 years.

Those six decades of research produced some very interesting results: The 1,528 geniuses had done fairly well. Many were professionals and had stable, prosperous lives. However very few had made notable creative contributions to society, and literally none of them had completed any extraordinary creative work.

Doctor Dean Simonton, the author of *Genius, Creativity and Leadership and Scientific Genius* says, "There just isn't any correlation between creativity and IQ." So much for that old "natural creative genius" myth.

So how do brilliant performers do it? What makes people like cellist Yo Yo Ma, psychotherapist Carl Jung and Albert Einstein so different?

Florida State University neuropsychologist Dr. Anders Ericsson has studied geniuses, superior performers and prodigies for over 20 years.

He's now convinced that geniuses and superior performers do *NOT* have any unusual inherited mental qualities. Ericsson says excellence in any field -- from the arts to business to sports -- comes from a willingness to "mentally stretch beyond one's conscious limits to gain access to deeper subconscious mental capabilities."

Genius is *NOT* necessarily a born condition. It can also be the end result of an individual's conscious effort to access their deeper subconscious mental capabilities.

During a recent interview the famed genius cellist Yo Yo Ma revealed his secret: "When I'm playing well," he said, "everything falls into alignment -- my physical self and my emotional self -- and I become focused in such a way that I actually have simultaneous access to both my conscious mind and my unconscious mind."

This same conscious-to-subconscious tie was also reported by the legendary psychotherapist Carl Jung. Albert Einstein also preferred a similar method of having conscious access to his subconscious mind. Consider Harvard researcher Jagdish Parikh's huge study, in which 16,000 high-level Fortune 500-type business executives credited 80 percent of their success to having "conscious access to their creative subconscious intuition."

How can you become more consciously aware of your subconscious materials and talents? On the surface this sounds impossible. Yet all of these brilliant creative people insist their secret is having conscious access to their subconscious mind.

Increase Your Natural Genius

How can you increase your own creativity and performance to your own genius levels? You now realize it's obviously important to have conscious access to your subconscious mind.

So ... let's take a look at what's inside your subconscious mind. Your subconscious mind operates quite a bit like a camera. Starting from birth it has recorded everything happening inside and outside of you 24 hours a day, both asleep and awake.

Being consciously aware of all this information would damage your ability to think clearly, or even survive. Your brain would be seriously overloaded, or at least distracted. So this massive amount of data is filed away in the subconscious mind for use on an "as-needed" basis.

How can you get conscious access to this huge storehouse of material? There are several ways to get direct access to your subconscious information, including: Intuition, engineered brainwave training audios, both regular and lucid dreams, creative breakthroughs, meditation, both hypnosis and guided relaxation, and spontaneous "higher consciousness" experiences.

Sharpen Your Creative Skills

Edward de Bono, an acclaimed creativity specialist, says, "Creative thinking is NOT a talent; it is a *SKILL* that can be learned. It empowers people by adding strength to their natural abilities."

So, how can you free your natural creative impulses? Stop and think about this for a moment. Remember how most of us were "hauled into conformity" by the educational system? How we were taught to sit quietly in our seats and ask permission to speak?

To free your creative impulse, start by rebelling against that old lesson. Overcome any impulse to just automatically "march in step" with the rest of humanity. Yes, this can be a challenge; but it is achievable. Kick-start yourself by seizing permission to rebel against those old constraints.

Get your creative thinking in gear:

Embrace Problems. You truly have countless opportunities to expand your creative thinking skills. Such opportunities present themselves daily at home, while driving to work, during meetings or lunch, or while just hanging out with friends.

The most basic approach is to recognize that a "problem" may actually be an opportunity for a creative explosion, then seize the opportunity and run with it.

Challenge Assumptions. It's totally natural and necessary to make assumptions about your everyday world. You would otherwise spend all of your waking hours in unnecessary mental analyses of ordinary things. But many times we see only what we expect to see.

Your brain's automatic analysis of a situation or a problem always starts by focusing on your past experience and beliefs. This can become so deeply ingrained that it suffocates your creativity.

This is why challenging your assumptions is such an important component of creativity. You can then look beyond the obvious and achieve valuable creative breakthroughs. At the same time you'll build a connection-rich brain that's even more unique and creative.

Truly creative people automatically challenge both their own assumptions and commonly accepted knowledge. This is the true source of all of the world's great inventions and businesses. The moment you choose to challenge an assumption, you are on the way to discovering something new and different.

Make Some Good Mistakes. Consider the great creative genius Edison, who held over 1,000 patents. Most of these patents are forgotten because they weren't worth much to begin with. But who is likely to forget the electric light? Don't let "fear of failure" keep you from exercising and building your creative muscles. Amaze yourself!

Bust loose of Old Limits. The essence of creativity is not necessarily getting things "right." At its heart, creativity is based on risk-taking – on being willing to make "mistakes."

Many who claim they are *not* creative just say this because they tried once, failed, and then gave up. *Interestingly, creative genius actually goes hand-in-hand with failure.*

Get Past Fear of Failure. The willingness to take risks is at the very heart of creativity. If you are unwilling to take risks and deal with what ordinary people call "failure," you can't expect to become a truly creative thinker.

No creative person succeeds without first failing. Failures are part of the process of testing our assumptions. Work to become comfortable taking risks. Each so-called "failure" you encounter will actually supercharge your creativity by generating new information.

Modern neuroscience has shown that our brains are actually physically rewired each time we learn something new by "making a mistake."

Try Alternative Thinking. Creating a new solution to an existing problem often requires looking at the problem from a fresh perspective. Many different tools are available to create a fresh perspective, including brainstorming and creative visualization. One simple and immediate way to kick-start your creativity is to look at your problem from the vantage point of another profession. If you're a mechanical engineer, for example, how would an architect view your problem? This often leads to some remarkable creative breakthroughs.

Get More Brilliant Insights

Jeri is sitting at home watching the Discovery channel. A light bulb suddenly flashes inside her brain. "Idea," it screams.

But the TV program is continuing, so Jeri just lets the idea go for later.

So... what happened to that brilliant idea that popped into her mind two days ago while driving to work? She also left that one "for later," and it too is now gone.

 Have you ever considered what your spontaneous ideas could become *IF* you paid attention to them? One of them might be the seed of the success you've long dreamed of.

Suppose that instead of being like Jeri, you jump into mental alertness and look more closely at your idea.

Suddenly another idea joins it, and you see a new possibility. Now you're experiencing genius-level creativity.

You have just had a creative "ah-ha" experience. Your brain fires up with excitement as you wrap it around your powerful thought or insight.

The spontaneous thoughts and ideas that just pop into your mind are *not* casual "accidents." A mysterious source of genius-level creative power is knocking at the door.

A New "Insights" Strategy

Have you ever heard someone say a great idea came to them "in a flash?" That's just what truly happened: A very real physical brain phenomenon is behind the sensation of a light bulb going off in your brain when you get a sudden creative insight.

Stop and think about the moments you have had such experiences. Do you recall being very relaxed?

Einstein claimed to get his greatest creative insights in the shower, where he could best "empty his mind." This is a major clue to these "light-bulb" ideas and insights.

The secret is this: Logical thinking uses a different part of your brain than creative thinking. Your brain can only do one or the other at any given time.

You must choose which mental state you wish to use --the analytical, or the creative. And the creative "mind set" depends on relaxation.

If you want to welcome a creative insight, start by asking yourself what activities tend to best help you "empty your mind?"

If you have a problem you're trying to solve, try this approach: First, exercise your logical analysis. Then just let go. Do something totally different and relaxing. Forget the problem. Let your subconscious mind play with the question or problem while you just go about your life and allow the insight to prepare to flash into your conscious mind.

A "Creative Brainstorming" Exercise

Just like exercising your muscles, your mind also works best if challenged with creative thinking exercises. Try the following creative brain-building technique.

First, Select your problem. Your subconscious mind operates 24/7 and is the source of almost all of your truly creative "ah-ha" ideas. Once you pose a question, it will go to work sorting through your lifetime of memories and insights looking for an answer.

Just before you go to bed, spend a half-hour or so contemplating your problem or challenge. Then when you turn out the light to sleep, just forget about it. **Second, carve out some time the next morning.** get up one hour before anyone else. Sit down in a comfortable chair with a cup of coffee or tea, a pad of paper, and your favorite pen or pencil.

Second, do an "idea dump." Just relax and let your ideas flow onto the paper. Write down everything down that comes to you—no matter how impossible or odd your ideas seem. Just let your brain do an idea dump and capture it for later evaluation.

Then...play with your ideas. Now (or later) playfully analyze your materials. Look for unique combinations or unusual insights. And look for how they all tie together into a single answer. Nine times out of ten you'll get a new creative insight.

Here are some ideas on how to analyze your materials: Most problems come in a cluster of smaller problems. List the related mini-problems that come to mind. Don't be critical at this point, just list everything that comes to mind.

Immediately increase your problem-solving skills a thousand-fold -- instead of asking "Is this the right answer?" ask "Is this the right *question*?" Look for both obvious and subconscious assumptions. Your subconscious assumptions may be connected to some interesting old personal fears that may have little or no basis in reality.

Look for a "solvable" problem on your list. Solving a smaller problem will often provide a string you can pull to unravel a bigger problem.

Dr. Jill Ammon-Wexler

FOUR. FEEL GREAT EVERY DAY

It's a warm Southern California evening in 1948. A freshly waxed and buffed purple Cadillac pulls into a nearly empty parking lot in front of California's prestigious Hollywood Bowl.

Wladziu Valentino steps out, wipes a spot from one of his gleaming white leather shoes, lightly tousles his hair, and adjusts a long paisley scarf around his neck.

He strides toward the office, scarf blowing in the light spring breeze, and opens the door with a flourish that would one day become his trademark.

He had dreamed for years of giving a concert in the Hollywood Bowl. The problem? He had never before played in the Bowl, and felt frustrated about his underlying fear of rejection. But Wladziu Valentino had a passion for his dream. So he wrote a check to rent the entire Hollywood Bowl for two hours on an off-night.

On the appointed night he showed up wearing a classic notched tails tuxedo and elegant ruffled shirt. He placed a huge candelabra on the piano with a flourish, then flung off his spotless white gloves, revealing a huge diamond ring on his right index finger.

He bowed to the rows of empty seats, flipped the tails of his tux and slid onto to the piano bench, then opened with a wildly energetic popular version of the Warsaw Concerto.

Two hours later he rose and took a bow to the spirited applause of the attending four man nightly maintenance crew. The flamboyant pianist strode from the stage with his head held high.

He had tasted the glory of his dream, and felt fabulous. Wladziu Valentino Liberace, later known only as Liberace, continued to build that dream. Four years later almost to the very night, he performed his first Hollywood Bowl concert to an outrageously enthusiastic standing-room-only crowd.

Anger Can Make You Happy

Emotion is one of the most powerful expressions of our human energy. It is literally mental energy in motion. And certain emotions are so powerful they can instantly change your life. Take anger, for example. Have you ever experienced rage? Then you have tasted the truly amazing power anger can have.

Most modern societies teach us that anger is negative, and that we should avoid or repress our anger. This does allow societies to better control their members; but is anger really negative, or is repression of anger just based on social convenience?

Do you feel somehow stuck in a rut or that your life is just running in a circle? Then maybe it's time to put some e-motion to work. Which human emotions have such power? Anger and love -- especially when fueled by the intense power of passion.

Not much needs to be said about the ability of passionate love to change your life. So how about passionate anger?

Actually hot, passionate anger is truly neither good nor bad. Anger is simply energy in motion. It's what you choose to DO with your anger that makes it a positive or negative force in your life.

How Anger Changes Lives

Here's a real story about the positive power of anger: "TR" was only in his early-twenties when he woke that morning, but he felt anything but great. He pulled on his shorts and socks, put on a pair of wrinkled pants and t-shirt, then sat on the edge of the bed and rubbed his eyes.

Life was not going well. He was overweight, burdened with debt, and totally without direction. He bent over to put on his shoes, but instead threw one at the wall. His pent-up anger rumbled to the surface, and he launched the other shoe at the wall. His face blazed crimson.

The frustration and self-loathing that had been building within suddenly erupted like a volcano. "This is enough," he shouted. "Enough! Enough, enough! I've had it."

Today this same man owns a multitude of successful businesses, and is highly regarded by millions of people around the world. "TR" (Tony Robbins) is a shining example of how you can use passionate anger to literally turn your life around on a dime.

Use Anger Positively

You have choices of how to use the energy of anger:

One, you can "stuff it" but your anger will NOT just go away. Repressed anger just makes a home somewhere in your body and creates disease. Have you ever asked someone, "What's eating you?" Your intuition picked up on their repressed anger. Repressed anger is at the heart of high blood pressure, ulcers, colitis, cancer, and a long list of nasty diseases and disorders. And yes, it truly does "eat" at us.

Two, you can turn it against others, but this strategy is obviously very counter-productive.

Three, you can "work it out" physically. Expressing the energy of anger through physical exertion is far more beneficial than "stuffing" it. Some common outlets are running, working out, dancing, etc.

Four, You can use it to motivate yourself. Think about what Tony Robbins did in his life. This is the same thing Eleanor Roosevelt did to transform herself from a homely, insecure young girl into a world respected leader. If your life isn't great, just get mad enough to change it!

Anger is just an emotion. But passionate anger can become a highly motivational, unstoppable energy. Put it to work in your life as a positive force!

"Fake" Yourself Happy

Liberace was quoted as saying, "Nobody will believe in you unless you believe in yourself." There's more than one way to feel great and be happy. You actually have more control over your moods than you think.

New research shows that people who simply choose to *ACT* more positive and outgoing DO improve their mood and overall outlook on life.

Let's take a closer look at the research done by William Fleeson, associate professor of psychology at Wake Forest University.

Fleeson had 47 students *act* either extroverted or introverted. The students then participated in a discussion group.

The researcher found that the students who simply acted energetic and assertive reported having significantly more fun than those who had agreed to act passive and shy.

"Simply acting extroverted makes people happier," says Fleeson "Every single participant in the study was happier when they acted extroverted than when they acted introverted. Even introverts can act extroverted and instantly become happier by changing their behavior," he explains.

"We tend to think of happiness as something that comes from outside us," Fleeson continues. "It's a radical idea that we have control of our happiness. But if people choose to ACT more outgoing, adventurous or assertive, they have the power to directly improve their own well-being. The research demonstrates that extroversion can actually 'cause' happiness."

Whether you want to become more out-going, quit smoking, achieve a business goal, create a fulfilling relationship, or simply feel great every day – the process is the same. Just picture it in your mind, then "act as if" you have already achieved your goal.

Expect some radical life-changing results!

Create Solid Belief

Successful people believe they will continue to feel great and be happy and successful. Unsuccessful people, on the other hand, subconsciously expect to continue to feel bad, to fail, and to be unhappy.

If you want to enjoy more happiness and success in your life, be sure your internal expectations reflect what you want. **"Acting as if" you're already happy and successful will build a subconscious expectation you will BE happy and successful.** This alone creates quantum leaps!

Other people respond to our actions. Act happy and successful and you'll be seen as being happy and successful. This will even further strengthen your belief! Liberace's success began as a dream, and he then began to act as if the dream was already true.

Acting as if is NOT "faking it." It creates a solid belief that then helps your brain guide your actions in an appropriate way.

How This Works

There are three interesting brain mechanisms behind the amazing power of "acting as if:"

First, your powerful subconscious mind does NOT logically question what you present to it. So it always accepts your "acting" as the literal truth.

Second, each time you "act as if" you are happy, your physical brain responds by building physical brain networks to support your "acting as if." What you are actually doing is changing your brain to support your desired reality.

Third, as you repeat your "act as if," your brain builds stronger and stronger brain cell-to-cell networks.

As the strength of these networks increases, your "acting as if" gains strength as an actual belief. And you know about the power of a belief!

Feel Great NOW

The research evidence is in. There's no doubt we each actually CHOOSE whether we will feel great, or instead feel discouraged and hopeless. Here are some strategies to choose the better of the two:

Stop Blaming. The minute you blame someone or something else for your problems or challenges, you throw away your own personal power. Release any habits of blaming anyone (including your own self) for current frustrations or unhappiness. Blame is unnecessary baggage. It just prevents you from moving forward and finding solutions to your challenges.

So you have made some mistakes? Actually a big part of our learning depends on making mistakes. Stop beating yourself up for your mistakes. No mistakes = zero personal growth. And zero personal growth = just more of the same in your life.

Pick a New Theme Song. If you're stuck in a rut in terms of how you feel about yourself, perhaps it's time for a new "theme song." Become aware of any tunes you hum to yourself in the back of your mind. You may discover a theme song – a message your subconscious mind is sending to you. If the message isn't totally positive, replace it with a more empowering and uplifting song.

Stop Looking Over Your Shoulder. You do NOT

have to deny any unfortunate things that happened to you in the past. BUT why would you choose to recreate and re-experience them in the present? You've already survived that old "stuff" and come out on top.

Leave the past in the past. You'll never rise above your past as long as you compare your present situation to the past. This keeps you just repeating the same old mistakes.

The past really only exists as we choose to recreate it in the present moment. Anyway, your past memories are actually only interpretations of what happened. They may or may not reflect the reality of what happened.

What would happen if you choose to stop letting your past limit you, and instead committed to focus on now? Focus on how you want your life to be NOW. Keep your eye on the road, instead of on the rear view mirror.

Get Some Exercise. University of Florida researchers have found that exercise is very beneficial when you feel negative, anxious or depressed. And they say this benefit is independent of whether your daily life events are positive or negative!

"We found that regardless of the events they experienced on any given day, [people have] an increased positive mood and a decreased negative mood on a day they exercised more," says Peter Giacobbi Jr., an assistant professor of sport and exercise psychology.

Laugh it Away. Laughter immediately lights up a special portion of your brain (the left pre-frontal cortex) that makes you a positive thinker. Laughter is a fabulous thing. A good laugh gives you the equivalent of 15-minutes of aerobic exercise, massages your internal organs, dissolves your stress, and generally makes you feel really great!

Here's a little laugh exercise for you: Your goal is to get a 5-minute belly laugh. Since many of us have had laughter conditioned right out of us, you might want to get started with a "fake" laugh. Yes, it sounds silly, but that alone is worth a laugh.

Just continue to fake laugh. *No chuckles* -- laugh as big as you can. Here's where the magic begins. Your brain responds to fake laughter by producing the "laughter neuro-chemicals" in your brain that tell you to laugh even more. So soon you'll find you've moved from fake to genuine laughter. And that is really worth a good laugh!

Now in the middle of your uproarious laughter, think about something that's been bothering you. Then go ahead and laugh about that too. Remind yourself that you have survived up to now, and this too shall pass.

Done laughing? Pull in a couple of deep breaths and appreciate the extra flow of oxygen into your brain. This is a little method that can help you feel great any time you choose. Get laughter into your life, and you'll get healthier and even live longer.

Dr. Jill Ammon-Wexler

FIVE. THE BUBBLE MACHINE

It was a mild April morning. My office manager burst into the office wild-eyed. Sally was never one to burst into my office, so she immediately got my attention.

"Dr. Jill," she grimaced. "John D. is out here, and he says he has to see you immediately. Now!"

"Don't I have someone scheduled for 9:15?" I asked.

"Umm humm," Sally nodded. "You're scheduled solid to 5:30. And John is NOT one of them."

John had been one of my executive clients for two months, so I told Sally to show him into the office for a quick meeting. But I was not prepared for what came through the door.

John, an "always impeccable" CEO of a promising

Silicon Valley company, was a mess. His suit was so rumpled it looked like he had slept in it … he was unshaven … and his eyes were puffy and rimmed bright red. My immediate thought was that someone very close to him must have suddenly died.

The next 15 minutes were hot and intense.

John related how a representative from an outside sales firm had proposed to sell his company's products. He was excited at the opportunity, glanced at the proposed contract, and signed it on the spot.

But yesterday, one week to the day, he discovered the contract had been a recipe for disaster. Just after lunch his Vice President of Sales, Bob, stormed into his office spitting fire.

Bob had discovered that John was paying the outside reps 33% more commission than his inside sales staff. The entire sales staff had quit and planned to sue.

John related how he had immediately grabbed the phone and called the outside company to cancel the contract. But he was rudely informed that they too would sue.

Both John and his company were now facing two multi-million dollar lawsuits. It was very possible his company would not survive, and John might also be personally wiped out.

He was shattered and confused.

How did this happen?

John admitted he had signed the contract without even reading it.

"But why, John?" I asked.

"Dr. Jill," he stammered. "I couldn't make any sense of the words on the paper."

So why was a man with advanced degrees in both Business and Engineering unable to read a contract? John was suffering from a common problem related to the "big S" -- stress. He was unable to focus his mind.

I had tried for two months to get John to commit to stress management training. But he kept insisting he "cooked" on the mental energy I peersonally refer to as "dangerously high chronic stress."

He could not read the contract for the same reason you cannot find your car keys when stressed. When your brain is focused in the survival-level brain stem, your higher thinking centers are essentially shut down. And chronic stress throws your focus straight down into the brain stem.

What Stress Is NOT

There's a common belief that intensely stressful multi-tasking lets you get more done in a shorter time. Many executives and entrepreneurs claim they do their best work when "cooking" with the mental and physical intense associated with the stress response.

Are they right? Actually, they aren't even close to right.

This is more than a myth, it's a dangerous mental and physical health mistake. The excitement that comes with intense stress is emergency power designed to get you safely through a crisis or threat. However this energy comes at a very real cost.

One cost is physical exhaustion leading to serious diseases and disorders. A second cost is the reduced intelligence that comes with the activation of your brain's survival center -- your brain stem. How about that as a great reason to slow down and focus?

Many people believe stress is caused by the events happening around them. But stress is NOT what's happening in the world around you.

Stress is NOT your boss coming at you with a scowl, or the heavy traffic driving home. It's NOT even learning you are about to lose your job, or even that your marriage is about to end.

Stress is <u>NOT</u> what is happening to you! Stress is your body's response to your *interpretation* of an event or condition.

How does this work? Your brain automatically responds to something you interpret as a threat by releasing stress hormones. These hormones make your heart race, speed up your breathing, contract your large muscles, dilate your pupils, and cause your liver to release glucose for increased energy.

Whew! You are now prepared to either fight or run.

This natural reaction is known as the "Stress Response." When turned on at the right time, it boosts your ability to perform well under pressure. BUT, it causes problems if it fails to turn off and then becomes chronic.

Good vs Bad Stress

Today's medical world tells us that stress is tied to many diseases and disorders. It is the DIRECT CAUSE of premature aging, and is also the known enemy of creativity, memory, learning, and optimal mental functioning.

Now stress is obviously OK if the driver in front of you suddenly slams on their brakes. And a little stress is OK if you are pumping yourself up to give a speech.

This kind of stress keeps you on your toes, and actually strengthens your immune system. It is also helpful when "dancing" with our rapidly changing world and weather patterns.

But the ongoing long-term stress that comes from struggling through a divorce, or fighting to keep your job in a down economy, can cause problems.

Pumping out stress hormones over an extended period wears down your body and brain -- often leaving you depleted, mentally dull, overwhelmed, and even physically sick.

Some of the signs of poor stress control include:

- Free-floating anxiety,
- A feeling you're under constant pressure,
- Irritability, anger, sadness or moodiness,
- Digestion problems or headaches,
- Frequent colds or flu,
- Mental dullness or depression,
- Problems understanding conversations,
- Sleeping disturbances or insomnia,
- Desire to overeat or drink too much alcohol, and
- Loss of interest in family or social contacts.

Chronic stress damages your brain, and especially your memory. Stress hormones send glucose, your brain's basic food, away from your brain to your large muscles. This reduces your ability to create or access your memories.

This is why some people cannot remember a traumatic event. It is also why those who reach old age after a lifetime of chronic stress often have a weak short-term memory.

Calm the "Monkey Mind"

Do thoughts often race non-stop through your mind? Such a "monkey mind" event goes hand in hand with both chronic and intense stress. Until you tame your monkey mind, you'll never be able to experience your true mental potential.

There's only one natural cure for the stress that feeds "monkey mind" -- the Relaxation Response. This natural body/mind state is the exact opposite of the Stress Response. It takes your body and mind into a peaceful feeling of calm well-being.

Some of the things that trigger the Relaxation Response include: Being in nature, gardening, walking, reading a good book, a hobby, spending time with a pet, a relaxing bath, sitting in the sun, or moderate exercise. Another increasingly popular method is brainwave training for INSTANT Zen-like deep relaxation.

Some methods you can use to get the upper hand on monkey mind include:

Meditation. Meditation could provide the answer you have been looking for. Anyone can meditate, regardless of their religious or cultural background. Meditation has been around for thousands of years, and has now been proven through scientific research to be a powerful stress buster.

As reported in a 2004 issue of Time Magazine -- brain scans prove that meditation actually shifts your brain's activity from the right side of your brain, over to the left side.

Such a shift calms your brain's often overworked "rational thinking center" and reduces the Stress Response. This shift of activity to the left side of the brain immediately allows you to be far more relaxed and mentally focused.

A joint study by universities in Wisconsin and Massachusetts measured the "right-brain/left-brain" balance of a group of people while they studied and practiced meditation over an eight-week period.

The research team reported that meditation stimulates left-brain positive moods and reduces stress. Dr. Giuseppe Pagnoni of Emory University's School of Medicine says people who undergo such

Dr. Jill Ammon-Wexler

training get "actual functional changes in their brain circuits."

Focused Contemplation. One great spin-off of meditation is "focused contemplation." This ancient tool has appeared down through the ages in almost all cultures. Focused contemplation simply involves holding your attention on a single object. The object of your focus could be:

- Your breathing,
- A spot on the wall,
- Engineered brainwave training audios,
- An image you visualize in your mind, or
- An image you look at, such as a candle flame.

If you have trouble concentrating, this approach could prove very useful. One very useful simple meditation method is to watch your breath. Here's how to do this simple meditation:

1. **Breathe deeply** – Consider starting with this technique if you have never tried focused contemplation before. Breathing is natural, and you don't really have to learn anything unusual.
2. **Pay attention to the flow of your breath** – Just notice how it feels as air enters and leaves

70

your nostrils. Don't try to follow it down to your lungs at first. When you feel your attention wander, just gently return your mental focus to your breath.

3. **Scan your body** – Focus on sensations like pain, tension, warmth or relaxation in different parts of your body. Combine body scanning with a breathing exercise, and imagine breathing heat or relaxation into and out of different parts of your body.

Guided Visualization. Many people prefer to relax by listening to guided imagery as a recorded voice directs them through a visualization exercise. Some excellent guided visualizations are available online and on CDs.

Yoga and Tai Chi. There are many physical practices that can turn on your Relaxation Response. Yoga and Tai Chi are popular methods of doing this; but actually walking, dancing, skating or any activity that gets you "out of your chair" cab have similar benefits. Pick one that naturally appeals to you.

Brainwave Training. Brainwave training takes advantage of your brain's natural tendency to "march in step" with regular sound stimulation such as music. If you have ever tapped your foot to music, you experienced brainwave entrainment -- the powerful secret behind modern brain training. Properly engineered brainwave training actually teaches your brain to create certain mental states on its own.

Dietary Measures. Your brain's most basic food is glucose. If you eat a well-rounded diet, you're providing your brain with a good supply of this fuel. If your brain doesn't get the glucose it needs, it simply cannot operate efficiently. Not only will you not be as smart as you should be, but your memory and judgment will suffer. The results can vary from mildly irritating to truly disastrous.

However if you suffer from chronic stress most of that fuel is going elsewhere. The Stress Response uses your brain's supply of glucose to prepare your body to fight or run.

This makes it hard to think under stress. Ever run in circles trying to find your car keys when you're in a hurry? This is also why chronic stress leads to very real brain exhaustion

Embrace Change

True, we do live in times of great unpredictable change. This alone can seem very stress-producing. But it is not what is happening around you that creates your stress. Your personal *response* to what is happening is what initiates your "Stress Response."

You basically experience stress because something has changed, and you interpreted that change as a threat to your well being. In regard to the challenge of change, remember this: You now know from quantum science that your very core IS constant change. Your body and brain are made up of the same changeable "quantum stuff" as the rest of the universe. The secret is to let yourself go and "flow" with today's rapidly changing world.

Habits and Stress

The best time to build your ability to de-stress is when things are relatively calm. This gives you a polished habit when life heats up. Good and bad habits are built by accumulated tiny daily choices. Each choice is stored in your subconscious mind on actual physical brain connections. String enough positive choices together, and you'll cement a positive habit with real staying power.

This is as true for "poor" choices as it is for "good" choices. By the time you realize you have either a good or a bad habit, that habit is physically embedded in your brain.

To change a habit, the first step is to become aware of it. Your next task is to change the daily practices that created that habit, and replace them with something more positive. But all of this must start with awareness and a decision.

Some positive new stress-busting habits to consider:

Take Control of Your Time. Small pleasures are major de-stressors but it's easy to forget to allow time for them. Make it a habit to avoid over-scheduling your life. If you feel stretched too thin, try eliminating something. Give yourself more time for the things you love to do, or that are truly the most important. This IS your life. Make the most of it!

Activate the Relaxation Response. Your body has two separate nervous system pathways it uses to turn on either stress, or relaxation. The physical opposite of the Stress Response is called the "Relaxation Response."

These two nervous system paths actually cancel each other out. So turning on the Relaxation Response is the fastest way to turn off the Stress Response.

It really IS that simple. Build a habit of getting some relaxation into your daily life. You will be happier, and will also live longer and healthier.

Forget Perfection. Are you trying to achieve perfection? This may seem a great goal, but can also "eat you up." Plus expecting perfection from others is a total waste of energy. If you simply love the taste of perfection, try limiting it to one part of your life. Then relax on the rest. Make it a habit to watch for and correct overemphasis on perfection. Learn to soar!

Watch Your Thoughts. Remember, it's your interpretation of what's happening that creates stress -- not what's actually happening outside of you. When feeling stressed, make it a habit to look at your interpretation of your surroundings.

You may not be able to control the environment around you, but you certainly can control how you respond. Your personal choices create what you call "your reality." Observe your thoughts and how they direct your actions.

Deal with Small Problems. Face your smaller everyday problems. Avoid letting them pile up. This alone is a very powerful stress management technique. Make it a habit to look at your problems as challenges rather than as problems. As you solve the little ones, your major problems will seem more manageable.

Get Past The Past. One of the greatest wastes of your personal energy is focusing on the past. Regretting past lost opportunities and events does nothing to change them. What it actually does is strengthen the brain networks holding them. This causes them to grow.

jRemember -- what we focus on grows. If what happened wasn't good then, how can remembering it make it good now?

Resolve to let that old stuff go. Focus on the positive instead of falling into negative thinking. Negative thinking limits you and just adds fuel to your stress.

Melt-Down at Home. We live in a fast-paced world. We rush to work on jammed freeways packed full of anxious drivers. We get to work and are surrounded by stressed bosses and co-workers. Then eight hours later we are again surrounded by blaring horns and tired, frustrated drivers. We arrive home exhausted and depleted.

Hopefully this is not true for your life. But it does describe many of the people you have to deal with.

Create a "melt-down" period when you get home. You otherwise risk spreading stress all over your close relationships. Take a couple of deep breaths before you go through the door. Make your home a relaxing, healing, stress-free haven!

Dr. Jill Ammon-Wexler

SIX. GO BEYOND "ORDINARY"

Early Sunday morning. You tossed and turned all night and it's now 5:18. Sleep is obviously impossible so you push yourself up out of bed and head to the kitchen for coffee.

Things are not going well lately. The company you work for is relocating to India. They have already started to outsource your duties. You should probably look for a new job, but where?

Your second cup of coffee moves you up a notch to semi-alert, so you go outside to get the Sunday morning paper.

The front page contains the usual gloom and doom headlines, and the Lifestyle section features tours to Africa and the Far East. "Fat chance of that," you think.

You sigh and think back five years ago when you were planning a trip to Africa with Steve, who was then your close business associate.

Your thoughts roll back. You and Steve were planning to open a high tech service business. You were to be VP of marketing. But Steve had been hurt in an accident on a hunting trip, and you somehow lost contact. "Too bad," you sigh. "I'd love to have that chance now."

You toss the Lifestyle section aside and turn to the Business section -- a part of the paper you lately use to line the garbage can. You flip to the second page and almost drop your coffee cup.

There as the "Business Man of the Week" is a picture of your old friend, Steve. He started the business the two of you discussed, and is now in his second year.

A couple of hours later you find his website and send Steve a congratulations email.

Then, much to your shock, you get an immediate email from Steve asking for your phone number. What happens that Sunday morning moves far beyond "coincidence." Steve offers you a dream job at a great salary, and suddenly your problems are solved.

Was all of this coincidence, or is some mysterious energy at work? Actually strange things happen to everyone. An old friend calls you up a minute after a distant recollection of them flashes through your head. Or someone suddenly pays you back an old debt when you truly need the money. What's this all about?

"Paranormal" is Normal

Do you doubt those stories about people seeing through walls, accurately predicting the future, traveling out-of-body or reading other peoples' minds? Many people assume these capabilities are a certain sign of an unbalanced mind, an overactive imagination, or just a stage trick.

Do these experiences have any reality? Are they just strange cases of coincidence, or even tricks? Or is there some truly solid truth behind paranormal experiences?

Many feel paranormal experiences lie outside the realm of scientific understanding. In some cases that may be true. But these experiences are not as mysterious as they once seemed. There's new evidence such peculiar gifts are far more common than we previously thought.

Apparently we ALL have ESP capabilities. The current scientific view is that paranormal abilities are a sixth sense that is just as normal and real as our other senses.

Is Someone Staring at You?

You're sitting at a table in an outdoor restaurant and suddenly have the sensation someone is staring at you. Your eyes are automatically drawn to a table to your left, and yes -- the man at the table is looking right at you.

On your way home you see a woman on the street that reminds you of an old friend. It's not her, but you're still thinking about her as you walk through the door. Seconds later the phone rings and it's the very friend you thought of.

Is all this simply coincidence, or is something else going on? Today's research indicates that at least seven out of ten of us have had the sensation of being stared at. Or we have thought of someone, only to have them call on the phone seconds or minutes later.

Far from paranormal, these experiences are rooted in our biology, says Dr. Rupert Sheldrake, a Cambridge-trained biochemist who feels our awareness is not restricted to the physical brain. He feels our brains reach out into "fields of influence" that are present throughout nature.

Sheldrake attributes mysteries like the synchronized flying of flocks of birds to a "shared collective unconscious" of that species.

To Sheldrake, telepathy is a natural unconscious communications field allowing distant members of a pack or tribe to stay in contact, or warn each other of danger. "Telepathy depends on social bonds," Sheldrake explains, "and the ability seems to be stronger in animals than in most people."

We humans have it too. The most common example of human telepathy is telephone telepathy -- sensing who is on the phone before you pick up the receiver. Sheldrake said this phenomenon is now also occurring with e-mail.

The probability is that YOU are experiencing this in your life. Is this evidence we humans also have a "shared collective unconscious?" That truly does fit in well with the current scientific theory that all of life is interconnected.

Walking Through Walls?

A rather ordinary-looking man wearing headphones sits in a small windowless room, a clipboard on his lap. His goal is to "see through the wall" and read a message in a sealed envelope located in a locked safe.

The "viewer" closes his eyes and goes into a state of deep relaxation. Suddenly his eyes pop open and he scribbles a note on the clipboard. Later that afternoon a Stanford Research Institute researcher compares the viewer's scribbled notes to the contents of the sealed envelope. For the 10th time in a row, he accurately described the envelope's contents.

Sound like a bizarre sci-fi movie?

Actually this is a very real scene from research funded for years by the US Government. For many years the CIA pumped millions into research projects like Project Stagnate, Project Grill Flame, and Operations Sun Streak and Stargate. When these project files were recently declassified, it was revealed that remote viewers had predicted the exact location of hidden Russian military targets. The accuracy of the viewers' reports was verified using satellite imagery.

Although it might sound like a "lunatic fringe" activity, remote viewing (RV) is being used today in criminal investigations and government intelligence work. It is even being used by businesses to predict the success of potential mining or drilling sites.

And, this may come as a surprise -- RV is NOT really "paranormal" at all. It is actually a learned skill. Many intelligent people who want to explore their full potential have become interested in developing their RV ability. And as might be predicted, training resources have become available to fill the demand.

Successful Executives Do It

The PSI Communications Project at the New Jersey Institute of Technology, formerly the Newark College of Engineering, has researched precognition since

1962. Over the years they have administered precognition tests to people in all walks of life and age brackets.

In terms of business people, the researchers report a very strong connection between high precognitive ability and superior management skill as measured by the superior profit production of top executives.

Your Odd Third Eye

A mysterious human "third eye" has been pondered by mystics through the ages, and has long been believed to be the source of a higher "inner vision." According to ancient traditions, when the third eye "awakens," one feels an unusual pressure at the base of their brain. This then creates a direct line of communication with "higher planes" of reality.

Is this just "ooh gum boo gum?"

You may be surprised to learn that such a "third eye" actually does exist. It is a tiny gland in your brain – the pineal gland. Your pineal is about the size of a pea, and sits in a tiny cave directly behind your eyes in the exact geometric center of your brain. And yes, it's real!

The pineal gland is believed to be the third eye. It is very similar to your normal eyes. It has a lens, contains a complete map of the visual field of your eyes, is activated by light, and controls your body's various natural biorhythms.

The pineal gland is now also known to respond to electromagnetic energy, and some researchers believe it may be actively involved in certain altered mental states.

At certain brainwave frequencies like deep Theta, a sense of our ego boundary often vanishes. Our consciousness is then less concerned with our "physical" state. According to many ancient traditions, this is when our "third eye" begins to exhibit special mental powers. And according to some recent research, the pineal may very well be involved in this experience.

The ancient mystery schools had their students first withdraw their attention from their physical senses. Many today say visualization exercises are helpful in activating your pineal gland-third eye connection. Whatever technique is used, the most interesting thing to note is that the pineal gland is most certainly real. As to its connection to higher states of consciousness — that is very much a personal experience.

Note: If this interests you, I have authored a popular Kindle book on the pineal gland third eye connection. The book includes detailed steps you can take to open your third eye, plus a remarkable 9-minute video lets you directly experience how it feels when you open your third eye. Review it here: http://www.BuildMindPower.com

Stretch Past "Ordinary"

You are most likely to have paranormal experiences in certain situations, including:

- During or after deep relaxation,
- During or after an extreme or sudden crisis,
- As part of a near death experience,
- Under anesthesia or psychedelic drugs,
- Due to sleep deprivation or exhaustion,
- During deep meditation or chanting,
- While firewalking or a shamanic ceremony,
- During a religious or higher states experience, and
- During engineered brainwave training.

Obviously some of these situations are more appealing than others. Few of us want to create an extreme or sudden crisis, approach death, fall into exhaustion, or depend on drugs or anesthesia just to have a paranormal experience.

Plus having a religious experience or attending a shamanic ceremony may not be appropriate. This leaves the options of visualization, brainwave training, chanting and meditation.

A Simple Meditation Experiment

If you have never experienced meditation, the following method will get you started. Just follow these simple steps:

1. Sit upright in a comfortable chair,
2. Keep your spine as straight as comfortable,
3. Position your feet flat on the floor,
4. Let your eyes gaze comfortably downward,
5. Soften your focus and do not "look" at anything in particular,
6. Let your eyelids "droop" as far down as comfortable,
7. Continue to gaze downward, focusing on nothing in particular,

8. Allow your breathing to become regular and comfortable,

9. Do not resist if your attention drifts. Just remain calm,

10.   If your eyes want to close, let them,

11.   Maintain your meditation for as long as you wish, and

12.   End your meditation with a few deep, slow breaths.

Sound Toning for Mental Clarity

Another proven method of creating the clear mental states associated with paranormal experiences is the use of sound. Certain sounds create actual steady (standing) vibrations in your brain.

In the *Mozart Effect*, vocal expert Don Campbell says that all forms of vocalization – including singing, chanting, and even talking – can enhance mood and memory.

"But nothing rivals toning" for higher states experiences, Campbell insists. "Toning goes back to the 14th century," he explains. "It refers to the process of making certain sounds using elongated vowels for extended periods of time."

According to Campbell, toning for 5 minutes a day for two weeks can produce some remarkable results. He reports that certain sounds tend to have very specific effects on the body and our emotions.

Try these tones...

Ahhh – Rapidly creates the stress-busting relaxation response.

Eee or Ayy – Are stimulating toning sounds. They aid concentration and release pain and anger.

Ohh or Omm – Is the richest sound. It warms your skin temperature and relaxes muscle tension. This is the classic sound used in several eastern disciplines to clear your mind.

Dr. Jill Ammon-Wexler

SEVEN. TURN BACK THE CLOCK

Julie pulls into a parking space marked "Visitor," sits motionless for a moment, then sighs and pulls a gift card and pen from her purse. She opens the card and writes, "Happy Birthday Mom. I love you, even though you don't remember who I am."

She picks up the bouquet of spring flowers on the seat next to her, grabs onto the string of a "Happy Birthday" helium balloon, locks the car, and walks slowly toward the front door of Rose Haven Extended Care.

She stops for a moment to breathe in the scent of the roses by the steps, and then goes somewhat reluctantly through the glass door.

The staff has dressed her mother, now waiting in a wheelchair by the window overlooking the rear garden. Julie puts on her best smile and walks toward her. The white-haired woman in the chair looks up in delight at the balloon, and then quizzically at Julie. "Hello dear," she says to her daughter. "Are you my new nurse?"

On the way home Julie detours to visit her great aunt Mary Madelyn, a Catholic Sister who is 17 years older than Julie's mother. She pulls in and immediately spots her aunt raking around the spruce alongside the old stone building.

"Julie, what a treat," the old woman beams. She pushes an escaped white lock back inside her straw hat, drops the rake, and holds out both arms to embrace her niece. "Come. Let's have tea," the old woman laughs with obvious delight.

What is happening to the older generation of women in Julie's family? Her 72-year old mother is in a care home for advanced Alzheimer's patients, while her 89-year old aunt is still mentally healthy. What cruel fate has struck here?

Why do some people get Alzheimer's disease, but still do fine mentally … while others simply go downhill and lose their mental capacity and memory?

Advantages of Older Brains

There's a myth in our modern society that aging brains inevitably lose their edge. Is this true? There's no doubt our brains are "snappier" in our youth.

However this leads to a very important question: Is it inevitable you will slow down mentally as you pass age 35? And what about the prediction that 50% or more of us will have Alzheimer's disease by the time we reach 80?

First, let's debunk the myth that older brains are less capable than those of the younger generation.

If you're having that "losing my marbles" fear, you'll be happy to hear what Duke University neuro-biologist Dr. Lawrence Katz has to say about our mental powers in the fifth decade and beyond.

Dr. Katz tells us we may be overlooking something very important. "In the old days, we called it wisdom," he says, "but what is wisdom, really? It is a dense and rich network of associations developed through a lifetime of experiences."

What's he talking about? As our brains age we do lose some of our mental processing speed. That is undeniable. But that "loss" is offset by more mature thinking strategies based on actual physical changes in our brain.

Doctor Katz is referring to a huge number of studies showing we get much better at problem solving as we age. "There's a reason we don't have 20-year-olds running Fortune 500 companies," he says.

He is only one among many researchers now convinced that the wisdom of age is based on a very specific brain condition. That condition is the same thing that sets geniuses apart from the "normal" population -- a rich network of brain cell-to-cell connections.

The aging brain does NOT need to fade. It can also contain a BUILT wisdom-creating rich neural network.

This explains why so many outrageously creative people seem to "bloom late." Apparently the brain needs to pack in a lifetime of experiences to create a Grandma Moses, a Socrates, or a Leonardo da Vinci.

What About Alzheimer's?

The renowned metaphysical author Aldous Huxley said, "The secret … is to carry the spirit of the child into old age, which means never losing your enthusiasm."

According to the Alzheimer's Association, as we reach age 65, ten percent of us will have some degree of Alzheimer's disease (AD). And it's also being predicted that over 50% of us will have AD by the time we reach 80.

Not good, considering our increasing life spans.

But here's the good news: Although you may not manage to avoid AD as you age, there are steps you can take NOW to lessen the mental damage if you do get it. The story of Julie, her mother, and her great aunt contains the seeds of a promising answer.

Julie's great aunt Mary Madelyn was a Teaching Sister who helped run a rustic school for impoverished orphans in Mexico. In many ways she is typical of a large group of nuns that have been studied for many years. Sister Mary Madelyn lived for years with two other Teaching Sisters. Their classroom was a *palapa* constructed by the local farmers, and the three lived in a crude plywood structure they called "home."

To entertain themselves after hours, the nuns played mentally stimulating games and created original Biblical crossword puzzles for one another. Now 89-years old, Sister Mary Madelyn has returned to California to enjoy her active and very happy retirement.

But why has Sister Mary Madelyn remained mentally sharp into old age, while her younger sister and Julie's mother – 17 years her junior – has been intellectually devastated by AD?

The Answer is the Brain

Doctor David Snowden walks up to the reception desk of Villa Assumpta -- an old mansion near Baltimore that houses 80 retired School Sisters of Notre Dame. Most of the retired Sisters are former school administrators and teachers in Catholic schools around Baltimore.

Over twenty years ago Dr. Snowden – today a neurology professor at the University of Kentucky

College of Medicine – began a research project studying 700 Catholic Sisters across the US. Over the years these Sisters have received annual physical and mental tests to measure the effects of aging. Many of them joke about the fact that the doctor will study their brains after their death.

Doctor Snowden pokes his head around one open door and smiles at 94-year old retired Teaching Sister Cecilia, who calls herself "one of the young ones." She greets him with a lively twinkle in her eyes.

Almost three quarters of the sisters have died since his study began; but interestingly, many lived to 100 and beyond without showing ANY signs of AD or dementia.

Snowden's team at first assumed that these mentally lively nuns had escaped AD. However autopsies revealed that their brains were actually riddled with AD plaque and tangles.

What Caused The Difference?

Why were these Sisters still mentally bright past 100 years, although their brains were full of Alzheimer's plaque? Snowden's study has been credited with an important research finding: A life filled with challenging intellectual activities and purpose seems to help defend against the negative mental effects of Alzheimer's disease.

The theory is that such activities build what scientists call a "neural reserve." Apparently having such a neural reserve can allow us to continue to have full mental capacity, even if we do get AD.

Your personal commitment to keeping your brain lively affects the way your brain responds to aging agrees Dr. David A. Bennett, director of the Rush Alzheimer's Disease Center.

He also refers to the benefits of a "neural reserve" -- the increased number of brain connections created by an active mental life.

Consider two people with similar amounts of AD deposits in their brain. The one with a personal history of enriched mental activities is significantly less likely to suffer the mental symptoms of AD, even though they have AD.

Do We "Think" Ourselves Old?

Do our thoughts make a difference in terms of keeping our brains sharp? Yes! We might actually "think ourselves old."

Does this seem unlikely to you? Then just imagine cutting a lemon in half, putting it into your mouth and biting down on it. Notice how your mouth immediately starts to produce more saliva? This is just one very simple example of how your thinking actually does physically affect your body.

Even looking at a picture of a lemon can cause your mouth to pucker.

How far can this go? To what extent does our mental and physical health deteriorate just because we expect it will?

A Yale University psychologist, Dr. Becca Levy, gave a group of people in their 60s and 70s a memory test. Before taking the test, half of the test subjects were exposed to negative words about aging, and half were shown positive words.

Are you surprised to learn that those exposed to negative words like "senile" did far worse on the test than those shown positive words like "wisdom?" This is only one example of research proving that if you believe getting older means losing your mental sharpness, you are actually more likely to do so.

"Old Dogs" and New Tricks

Just a few years ago science was convinced that our mental potential was "set in cement" once we reach adulthood. That is no longer believed to be true! Today's remarkable high-tech brain study devices have turned that old theory upside down.

Although it's not yet possible to totally age-proof our brains, new research holds out hope. Science now knows that our brains continue to physically change and grow throughout our entire life. What does this mean? Read on!

Brain deterioration caused by aging is NOT inevitable. [The brain's] design features are such that it should continue to function for a lifetime," says Dr. Zaven Khachaturian, director of the Alzheimer's Association's Reagan Research Institute. "There's no reason to expect it to deteriorate with age."

So, what is the secret to keeping our brains agile and fit? For over ten years a huge team of scientists has studied the genetic, psychological, social, and environmental factors related to mental fitness.

Dr. Marilyn Albert of Harvard Medical School and researchers at Yale, Duke, and Brandeis Universities and the Mt. Sinai School of Medicine examined 1,192 healthy and mentally fit individuals between ages 70 to 80.

They found that four factors tend to maintain one's aging mental fitness:

- Educational levels,
- Physical activity,
- Healthy lung function, and
- Feelings of self-confidence.

"Each of these elements alters the way our brain functions," says Dr. Albert.

Education. Apparently education improves our brain function by directly stimulating our brain cells. "If you have a lot of neurons and keep them busy, you may be able to tolerate more damage to your brain before it shows," says Dr. Peter Davies of New York's Albert Einstein College of Medicine.

The important point to remember is that the benefits of education can be gained at any age -- a good reason to return to the college campus regardless of how "old" you are.

Physical Activity. Many studies confirm that both mental and physical activity boost brain fitness. Psychologist William Greenough of the Beckman Institute for Advanced Science and Technology provided some laboratory rats with a surplus of rat toys.

The rodents promptly developed 25 percent more connections between their brain cells than normal rats. Greenough reported that rats who were also exercised on a treadmill developed more capillaries in their brains, increasing the blood flow to their brains.

It may surprise you to learn that even walking will make you smarter! Mature adults who engage in a regular walking program improve significantly on tests of their higher level mental functions.

Mild aerobic exercise like walking raises the level of an important brain chemical – neurotrophic factor, or BDNF. This protects your brain cells from free-radical damage, builds the number of connections between your brain cells, and improves blood circulation in your brain.

Mental Activity. The most basic way to build your mind power is to challenge and exercise your brain. You can create healthy new brain cell connections by learning a new skill or language, or even through the stimulation of longevity-focused brainwave training. Even so-called "physical" activities such as yoga, Tai Chi, skating or dancing, or physical workouts actually build brain power.

Some other things that will increase your "neural reserve" include regular moderate exercise, frequent social interaction, and a healthy diet.

The less obvious side of the picture involves just doing familiar things in unusual ways. Simply changing your regular routines can provide tremendous stimulation to your brain.

Get Started Today

Here are a few very simple ways to stimulate your brain to increase your healthy neural activity level:

Change Your Inner Map. Rearranging the furniture is a sure way to stimulate your brain. Even a little change like putting your toothbrush on the other side of the sink will force your brain to create new pathways. And a lot of little changes can really shake things up!

Do Puzzles and Games. Many, many studies have shown that doing crossword puzzles or playing games like Scrabble, Chess and cards will sharpen your memory and language skills. And assembling jigsaw puzzles creates new brain pathways related to your spatial intelligence.

Reverse Your Dominance. Try using your non-dominant hand to do ordinary things like opening a cupboard or drawer, or perhaps brushing your hair or teeth. For a really tough challenge try buttoning your blouse or shirt with one hand, or even transfer your mouse to the other side of the computer. These may seem like little things, but they force your brain to create valuable new connections.

Read Out Loud. Take turns reading aloud to another person. Both reading out loud and active listening promote healthy interaction between your brain's left and right hemispheres.

Share Your Insights. Pay attention to what's happening around you, and share your insights with another person. This will have a dramatic positive effect on both your attention and memory skills.

Laugh. A great way to slow the aging process is laughter. Laughter protects your nervous system and gives your endocrine system a much-needed rest, all at the same time. When you laugh you boost your immune system, clear waste products out of your internal organs and tissues, and increase the oxygen in your body and brain at both cellular and organ levels.

It is also interesting to note that cancer cells die in the presence of oxygen. So if nothing else, at least get a good laugh about something.

Build Your Confidence. A sense of self-confidence can help protect your brain from the damaging effects of stress. There is strong evidence that elevated levels of stress hormones damage, and even kill brain cells. Stress has been proven to cause the hippocampus – part of the brain crucial to memory – to physically shrink.

As you learned in an earlier chapter – stress is NOT caused by external events. It is the result of your responses to what is happening around you. A high level of self-confidence increases the belief you are in charge of your own life, and can handle what's happening around you.

Building your self-esteem and self-confidence thus helps retard the release of stress hormones, protecting you from the aging process.

Pursue Healthy Longevity

George Burns, a comedian who lived to a healthy 100 years, said, "The single most important key to longevity is avoiding worry, stress and tension. And if you didn't ask me, I'd still have to say it." It's never too early, or too late, to start a healthy longevity routine. Here's how to get started:

Drink More Water. By the time you're thirsty you are already dehydrated. Research proves your IQ actually drops from 20 to 50% due to dehydration.

And note that coffee, tea and cola do NOT count!

Get Some Regular Exercise. The natural mood-enhancing brain chemical beta-endorphin is a key player in how exercise protects our brains as we age. "We now know that exercise helps generate new brain cells, even in the aging brain," says Dr. Fred Gage of the Salk Institute for Biological Studies.

Your brain needs a good supply of oxygen-rich blood to perform at its best. Even a short walk will feed your brain, but a regular physical workout will do even more.

Stretch Your Brain. Your brain follows the same rule as your muscles -- use it or lose it. Unused connections between your brain cells, just like an unused path through a meadow, will eventually disappear.

But if you do regular mental workouts, the connections between your brain cells will survive and strengthen – just like using a path through a field on a regular basis.

Plus if you "overload" your brain every so often, you can force it to physically reorganize itself and grow.

This is the mental equivalent of the muscle overload techniques used by body builders to build strong, healthy muscles.

The right kind of mental overload leads straight into quantum brain growth. If you simply provide your brain with a diet of unchallenging information, on the other hand, it will actually physically shrink. Two great growth-promoting mental exercises are learning a second language, or learning to play a musical instrument.

Doctor K. Anders Ericsson, a psychology professor at Florida State University strongly recommends you challenge yourself mentally. "Getting good at something is hard," he says. "If you can't do something it's not because you're old, but because you're not willing to put the time in on it."

He cites a study in which researchers read off a series of numbers, one per second, to a group of college students. When they began the experiment, the best students could repeat up to 25 numbers. At the end they could repeat 80 or more digits.

Do you think age is a determining factor? In July of 2005, 59-year-old Akira Haraguchi recited pi to

83,431 decimal places -- setting a world record for people of any age.

Boost Your Brain Power. You can also boost your brain power with professional brainwave training. This can actually train your brain to create such positive states as: Instant stress reduction, monk-like deep meditation, sustained motivation, rapid learning, enhanced memory, and crystal clear mental clarity.

This teaches your brain special skills that would normally require years and years to develop. Certain brainwave training scenarios also have such specific effects as: Stimulating the release of longevity-producing human growth hormone -- reducing headaches, and increasing healing.

Eat Brain-Smart Foods. Are there any magic bullets that can help protect your mental vitality into old age? Yes. There is a lot of evidence that the right diet and certain remarkable supplements will help keep your brain young.

Researchers at the Human Nutrition Research Center on Aging at Tufts University investigated food as a means of preventing age-related mental declines.

They began with deeply colored fruits and vegetables like blueberries and carrots, which are packed with the natural antioxidants that fight free radicals and inflammation in the brain. For two months they fed fruit and vegetable pellets to 19-month-old rats that were showing signs of aging, declined motor function, and weakened memory.

The effects were dramatic. The rats' motor function and memory improved significantly, with the most dramatic changes in those who ate blueberries. The rats that ate blueberries (and to a somewhat lesser extent the other foods) actually had physically healthier brains.

There are many, many studies that prove that fruits and vegetables contain thousands of compounds offering protection against mental decline, and even against Alzheimer's disease. And new studies are also pointing to the importance of a good supply of healthy fats in our daily diets.

Control Your Stress. I remember hearing family stories about how my great aunt Minnie "turned white" overnight in her mid 30s. This really did happen. The cause was extreme stress following the sudden death of her beloved husband.

If you have ever blamed stress for new wrinkles or gray hairs, you were probably right. There is now strong proof that long-term or sudden intense stress makes us grow old before our time. But there is also proof that a positive outlook can greatly reduce the impact of stress on your health. It cannot ravage your body if your mind says "no."

Doctor Elissa Epel of the University of California at San Francisco studied women suffering from the intense stress of caring for a chronically ill child. Her study looked deep inside the women's cells to determine if stress was affecting a key part of their chromosomes called a "telomere."

Telomeres cap the ends of the chromosomes containing your body's DNA, and are recognized markers of aging. As people get older this cap gets ground down. When the telomere gets too short to work properly, cells all over your body start to sicken or die. That's when the diseases of old age begin to set in.

Doctor Epel's research team discovered that the longer a woman had cared for a child with a serious illness, the shorter her telomere. "They had lost the amount of telomeric DNA one would expect to lose in

10 years of aging," Dr. Epel says. But the women in Dr. Epel's study who viewed their situation positively did not suffer the ill effects of stress.

"A positive outlook on life, a regular stress-management regime, and the support of friends can help buffer the potential damage of ongoing stress, she says. Dr. Gary Small, professor of psychiatry and behavioral sciences at UCLA, agrees, and says: "We have absolute evidence that people can preserve their memory by adding stress reduction to their daily routine,"

Learn the Tango. The hot and sexy moves of the Argentine Tango not only keep the aging body in shape, they may also sharpen the brain. Researcher Patricia McKinley of McGill University recruited 30 seniors ages 68 to 91 for an unusual study. Half the group received tango lessons, and the other half were assigned to a directed walking group.

The dancers got an almost immediate boost in their self-esteem. At first "they came in with sweatpants and sneakers, but after the third or fourth class, they had on makeup and jewelry," McKinley says. The class was mostly older women, but also included many older men.

After 10 weeks both the walkers and the tango dancers had better scores on memory tests. But only the tango dancers improved on a multi-tasking test. Such a boost translates to better abilities off the dance floor such as the ability to talk on the phone while responding to an e-mail.

The tango dancers also gained improvements in balance and motor coordination. This suggests they'd be at less risk of falling – a significant gain for older people, McKinley says.

Breathe Deeply. The importance of healthy lung functions cannot be over emphasized. If you don't exercise vigorously enough to cause yourself to take deep breaths, consider a simple deep breathing exercise every day.

Dr. Jill Ammon-Wexler

EIGHT. WHAT DO YOU WANT?

Robert and Jim graduated from UCLA in 1997. The two had a lot in common. They each majored in business, had solid academic "B" averages, were popular members of the varsity football team, and belonged to the same fraternity. They were, in fact, very close friends.

The two men still have a lot in common. They both live in San Jose, California -- and are married with two children. They even work at the same company. But that's where the similarities end.

One of the men, Robert, is the company President and is now a multi-millionaire.

The other man, Jim, is the Customer Support Manager, has a little money in the bank, and his family is relatively comfortable because his wife also works full-time.

What made these men's lives so different? It's no accident Robert is a company president. He chose to create the company himself eight years ago – only two years out of college. He had a vision of "a different service company," set his goal, and went to work to manifest it. Was it easy? Of course not. But Robert had a vision and absolute determination.

Jim also had a dream. But even before college Jim's passion was designing and building small sailboats. He was actually very good at it. One of his boats still consistently wins the Wharf-to-Wharf race in Santa Cruz, and the skipper of the boat once offered Jim financing to go into the boat-building business.

However Jim has always looked upon his one-time passion as "a kid's hobby," and feels he can't really afford to seriously pursue it. So … a partially built boat sits in the backyard – untouched for three years – and Jim continues to work at his "job."

What created such different paths for these two men? Robert listened to his heart's desire. He stepped into the face of very possible failure and took a leap. Jim, on the other hand, turned from his passion in favor of a sense of "security." He today feels bored and restless, but still refuses to "waste his time" designing and building sailboats.

Stuck in a Box?

Do you feel bored, restless, or dissatisfied with the direction of your life? Many assume this is not a good thing. It can't be denied that such feelings have the potential to wear you down, and maybe even seem to dampen your enthusiasm for life.

Actually if you are feeling bored, restless, or dissatisfied with the direction or circumstances of your life, this CAN be a very positive sign. It may indicate you're positioned at a major turning point in your life -- your "box" has become too small!

You know what a box looks like. It has four sides, a bottom, and usually also a top. It's made to contain something within its limits. So what do I mean when I say that if you're feeling restless and dissatisfied, it could be because your box is too small?

Each of us really does create our own box in the form of a set of limits for our life. These limits are based on our beliefs about our past experiences, and the rules we then create for ourselves to avoid future pain and failure. Your box places very real limits on what you want, and how to get it.

So, if you feel sick and tired of feeling boxed in by your past choices, your subconscious mind is telling you it's time to bust out. You may, in fact, be ripe for a quantum leap!

How Success Happens

Here's a BIG SECRET you need to remember about breaking out of your box and creating new levels of success in your life: Achieving a goal is NOT what makes you a success. Success is the process of becoming the person to whom your goal belongs.

Success is *NOT* achieving a goal! Success is the PROCESS of *becoming* the person that your goal belongs to!

Think about that young man who became a successful company president. He was actually a success the day he absolutely committed to go for it.

From that day forward each step he took changed him. He finally became the president of a successful company.

So how can you become a success? By choosing to focus your daily life on achieving a worthwhile goal, and then committing to take the daily steps to become the person that goal belongs to. This is true for goals in any endeavor -- business, personal, relationship, creative, spiritual or social.

If you want to be physically fit, for example, you could start with an absolute commitment to your own fitness. Then you would make it a daily goal, and focus every day on regular exercise and healthy eating habits.

If your goal is having your own million-dollar business, your daily focus could be to develop the skills and attitudes of a millionaire business owner.

If your goal is to get a big raise at work, your daily focus could be to become the type of employee that raise belongs to!

121

Food For Thought

Here's some food for thought: What do you think the daily lifestyles of current mega-successful people were like as they became successful?

Do you think Oprah spent five hours every night watching TV? Or Anthony Robbins sat around drinking beer with his buddies and watching sports videos? Or Tina Turner spent her evenings eating potato chips and reading magazines? Or how about Bill Gates spending his afternoons taking 3-hour naps?

What's happening in your day-to-day life? Do you want one year from now to be exactly like today? No? Then what do you want one year from now? What is your dream? Do you have one? One year from now you will be one year older. But will you be happier and more successful? And how about ten years from now?

Here are some very real stories:

Mary Walker in Florida celebrated her 60th birthday just over six years ago. The morning after her 60th birthday she says she woke up feeling out of sorts. "I suddenly had to ask myself what I'd done with my life," she recalls. "I spent all those years as a secretary, when what I dreamed of was being an interior decorator."

Mary then did the unthinkable. Against the loud protests of her 42-year-old daughter, she enrolled in a nearby university to study interior decorating. She is today a partner in a successful Tampa design studio, and says she "feels like a kid in a candy store."

Mike Deluca in Arizona was a hard working independent insurance broker who used to get home after long work days and just want a beer and TV time. But eight months ago a new challenge pushed Mike right out of his comfort zone. A national insurance brokerage with a huge advertising budget opened an office two doors down from his office.

Mike could see the handwriting on the wall. After a week of wrestling with his harsh new reality, Mike had a breakthrough. He decided to carve out a niche that the big firm wanted nothing to do with – insuring manufactured and mobile homes.

Using the services of an online consulting firm, two months later Mike was the author of a book on how to protect the value of manufactured and mobile homes. He offered free copies to potential new clients, and his business immediately boomed.

Get "On Purpose"

So ... are you a single working mom with few opportunities to create a dynamic new reality? And you are waiting until the kids are grown and you "have your life back?" Humm. What if you carved out one hour a day to explore your passion? Over a month that actually equals 30 hours — almost four 8-hour days. What could you do with that time?

Or are you a guy that just wants "TV and beer time" at the end of the day? Two hours a night less TV and you'll have 60 hours a month to start your own business, or even write that book you've dreamed of writing. How could authoring your own book supercharge your professional or business potential?

Get Started. Consider taking advantage of your restlessness and break outside your box. Here is a strategy to get you started. Ask yourself the following questions:

- How long have I been in this box?
- What's different today?
- Why is my box now too small?

Talk through the answers with yourself. This IS your life. Why not turn up the power and have more happiness and satisfaction? Why not do something that will help make one of your dreams come true?

We all have untapped ability and potential just waiting for us to choose a direction and take action. You're no exception. Commit to action — don't wait until you "feel better." That's just the procrastinator's trap. Do something radically different right now!

Decide What You Want. If you feel limited in any way, it's time to turn on your mental headlights and find an answer. The following exercise will get that process rolling. Grab a pencil or pen and answer the following questions. The act of writing leads to powerful new insights you will never get by just "thinking about it."

1. What do I really want?
2. Why do I want this?
3. Who do I want it for?
4. Why?

5. What do I assume is possible?
6. What do I assume is impossible?
7. Do I truly expect to get or achieve this? Why or why not?

Clarify Your Desire. Napoleon Hill said, "If your desires are strong enough you will possess super-human powers to achieve." The greater your desire, the stronger your will to pursue your goal. This is the very reason you want to select a goal you strongly desire.

Takes some time to look into yourself and prioritize the important aspects of your life. Consider your health, relationships, work, travel, culture, education, family, friends, financial status, children, sports, recreation, etc.

Go ahead and work it out on paper. It makes more sense when you do so. Be as specific as possible about exactly what your desired end result is. See what ends up on the top of your list. What will achieving that goal really look like?

Success requires mental clarity. If your goal is to create a successful business, ask yourself what that business will be? Are you thinking of simply hiring someone else to give you more free time? Are you looking for a very specific monthly profit? Or can your goal be best expressed in terms of a certain lifestyle?

Clarify exactly what you want in as much detail as possible. Yes, this is hard work. But without a clear mental picture, you will never have the focus required to achieve your goal.

Identify Your Resistance. About 80 percent of what holds us back is internal. The remaining 20 percent is in the outside world. And even then, it's our personal internal responses to what's outside that determines if we will succeed.

Your internal "resistance" controls what you can (and cannot) achieve in your lives. Unless you identify what is holding you back, you will never overcome it. And the really interesting thing is this: most of your internal resistance is probably just "old stuff" you have dragged forward from childhood. It often has no real truth for who you are today.

Superior achievers often ask one question when they are not moving ahead: "What am I doing or thinking that's holding me back?" Demand an answer. You need to know how you are placing limitations on yourself. Ask focused questions. The more intense and honest your questions, the more insight and ideas you'll generate.

Take Action. What can you do if you still lack clarity? One way to get into action is to simply make a choice from among your unknowns. Whether or not your choice is the "right" choice, just take at least a small step in what seems to be the best direction.

Here's what I have learned in my own life: Movement in any direction will break you free from the cement of indecision, and provides new information and experiences.

If you find you've stepped onto the wrong path, you can always adjust your direction. And any so-called "mistakes" will simply add to your personal wisdom about what doesn't work—taking you closer to discovering what does work.

There is great power in action. Action sends ripples of energy and change out into the world. And since life is so totally unpredictable, who knows how your situation will change once you get some action energy into motion.

ACT Like a Winner

Albert Schweitzer said, "Success is not the key to happiness. Happiness is the key to success. Love what you are doing ... you will be successful." The following tips will help you get on target and act like a winner – the path that will take you to the "winner's circle."

 **Light a Fire in Your Belly.** Your basic goal is to BECOME the person your goal belongs to. Do this by ACTING like that person!

As you become that person, your goal will manifest around you. This is perhaps the least understood rule of how success is actually created!

Start by making sure you have the right goal. What do you really want in your life? If you could be or do anything, what would it be? What is your compelling reason for wanting this? What drives you? If you can't pinpoint exactly what you want, daydream and see what comes up.

To achieve a big goal you must want it so much that it becomes a burning desire – a fire in your belly! Persistence is then virtually automatic.

Do you have a passionate, burning desire to achieve your goal? Do you feel excited? Do you really want it? If not, it may not be the right goal for you. Make up your mind. Without emotional fire and desire, it's too easy to quit at the first bump in the road.

Commit to Peak Performance. If you want something more than what you have today, you will have to DO something more. This doesn't necessarily mean working harder or longer. But it probably will mean working smarter and more passionately. Lasting success springs from attitudes that carry over into your entire life. Make passionate peak performance a daily habit.

Get Focused. Successful people have learned to avoid focusing on problems. Refuse to give attention to anything that seems to indicate your goal can't be achieved. Focus on what you want, not on what you don't want!

By regularly visualizing the result you desire, your subconscious mind begins to accept it as already real. Consistent daily focus is absolutely necessary to stabilize the new brain pathways connected to your goals. Without daily focus, the old mental habits that have kept you from your goal up until now will just take over again.

Get Organized. Successful people know that space management is just as important as time management. They have organized desks and files, and organized day timers or schedules.

If you want a higher level of success, spend some time getting your creative space organized, and then make it a priority to keep it that way. It is almost impossible to have an orderly, efficient brain in a cluttered and disorganized space.

Get Connected. Get out and meet other people in your field. Find them on the web and get to know them. Create or become part of a Master Mind group—a group of people committed to helping each other become successful. Meet once a week (even on the telephone) to brainstorm ideas, and give advice and support to one another.

Avoid negative people. Not too much can be said about this. Some people tend to seek out the negative aspects of literally everything. Do not let such people influence your thinking.

Bust Your Stress. It's very important to do an honest evaluation of your stress level. Stress can have a very negative impact on your brain because sress: (1) kills brain cells, and (2) focuses your mental activity in parts of the brain that do NOT support productive creative thinking.

Super successful people know how important it is to have a balance in their life. Bill Gates takes an entire week off each month and seeks solitude to clear his mind. But just as important as personal retreats is some play time with your family and friends. Take some time to get de-stressed, and you'll be far more productive and creative.

Stay Positive. Successful people have strong self-images. They have a sense of their own self worth, and are confident they can handle whatever life tosses in their path. If you have personal doubts, that's the first place to start on your pathway to success. This must be dealt with, or you will just continue to have the same problems that have held you back in the past.

Avoid being your own worst critic and rubbing your own nose in the dirt. Every project and undertaking has its ups and downs. The winners learn from their so-called failures and mistakes, and use that knowledge to take a step up. I'm convinced that all successful people literally "fail" their way to success.

I'm not saying they necessarily enjoy their failures. I know I never have. But failures truly are an essential step on the road to success.

After all, if it was that easy to be a big success, anyone could do it. True success takes guts, persistence, and the ability to get up and go on after you trip over a bump in the road.

Focus On Today. What you do each day moves you either toward, or away from, the goal you desire. You will have the success you desire if you adopt a daily lifestyle committed to achievement. Achievement is built by taking one small action after another. Your daily actions literally create your destiny.

If you commit to take at least one small action each day, your actions will add up and make a difference. Avoid sitting back waiting for that big second when everything will magically "just happen." That day will not come. Success happens one day at a time due to unwavering and persistent daily personal efforts.

Stay Passionate. One of the most powerful success tools is having a burning passion for your goal. You already know about the power of intense emotion and the huge impact it has on your brain. Intense passionate desire for your goal will help you create strong and durable new brain cell-to-cell pathways.

Many, many scientific studies have shown that intense passion is a key success tool. Don't try to force something to happen. Go for the type of inspired, joyful action that comes from pursuing a goal that's in true alignment with your dreams. This will help your life flow along easily and with far less struggle.

Persist. In many cases persistence is the only quality separating highly successful men and women from everyone else. If you were to select just one aspect of your personality to develop, I suggest you put persistence at the top of your list.

In his classic book *Think and Grow Rich*, Napoleon Hill felt so strongly about persistence he devoted an entire chapter to it. Hill tells us that, "There may be no heroic connotation to the word persistence, but the quality is to your character what carbon is to steel."

Consider what Hill is saying: Just as carbon hardens steel—persistence hardens your willpower. Persistence enables you to turn up the power and blast past any obstacles you hit while pursuing your dreams. You want this as part of your character.

Dr. Jill Ammon-Wexler

NINE. FLOW INTO HIGHER STATES

He walks quietly onto the stage totally unaware of the audience. The auditorium becomes extraordinarily quiet as thousands of people seem to hold their breath.

The slender, calmly intense man adjusts the chair in the center of the stage about one inch. He removes the gleaming cello from its stand, then gracefully sits and cradles the instrument with the finesse and familiarity most of us reserve for our very special loved one.

There is a brief elongated moment of silence as he closes his eyes.

The audience explodes into applause as Yo Yo Ma's bow coaxes the cello into song. The greatest cellist of our time has opened a concert in Vienna's historic Hofburg Imperial Palace.

~~~~~~~~~~~~

Simultaneously thousands of miles away in Berkeley, California, an intense 11-year-old girl leans against the barrier encircling the Iceland Skating Rink and closes her eyes. A look of peaceful, ageless wisdom comes over her face. When her clear blue eyes snap open, they seem to look into another time and place. She leaps forward on the ice, builds superhuman momentum, and gracefully catapults her body into the air in a perfect triple axel.

~~~~~~~~~~~~

At the same time across the world in a 16th century apartment above Amsterdam's Raamgracht Canal, a woman brushes a stand of white hair from her cheek, straightens her back, takes a deep breath, positions her hands over a worn keyboard, and allows the last chapter of a deeply moving novel to flow through her finger tips.

~~~~~~~~~~~~

In Komaki, Japan a man pushes away from his desk, loosens his tie, and heads for the elevator. We watch as he walks into a nearby park, settles onto a bench, then folds his hands and closes his eyes. He seems to be sunbathing, and is unaware of the scream of a jet taking off from nearby Nagoya Airport. But suddenly he sits upright, pulls a pad from his jacket pocket, and excitedly jots some notes.

"Higher States" Are Attainable

You've heard how musicians lose themselves in their music, athletes go into a trance to mentally rehearse their moves, brilliant inventors or business people "stumble upon" brilliant ideas, and writers and painters "become one" with their creations.

Can the rest of us have this remarkable experience? It's a common myth that such remarkable mental states and levels of achievement can only be reached by a few gifted people. *BUT is this true?*

If you've ever seen a high achieving athlete "in action," you know how spellbinding it can be. They seem to almost defy the natural laws of nature. Just what are they doing? Why do they get that calm look on their face as though they are in another dimension? And why do so many of these people say that time stops, and only their current activity remains?

Modern neuroscience tells us that such states of awareness are a normal brain state – but one in which we no longer focus on our ordinary sense of our self as connected to a physical body or time.

Does that sound strange to you? Many researchers say our most important discoveries, highest peaks of ecstasy, and greatest moments of inspiration and personal performance occur during such higher mental states.

YOU may have had such an experience of being outside space and time ... of reliving your past or the past of an ancestor or other person ... of having vivid imagery of mythical or religious symbols ... of undergoing an intense illumination and dissolving into pure energy ... of leaving your body ... of feeling at one with God or a divine being or energy ... of setting an unbelievable personal record, or having an intense experience of just "knowing" something.

The Secret of Entering "Flow"

There's a shared secret among super achieving performers, spiritual adepts, artists, athletes, inventors and geniuses in all fields. These remarkable people enter into one of the most enjoyable and valuable "super-conscious" experiences possible. It's commonly called "entering the flow."

Here's an example:

A batter walks up to the plate and gets ready for the pitch. Eighteen seconds later the spectators barely see the pitched ball rocketing toward the plate at 101 miles an hour. But to the batter, the ball seems to float slowly toward him looking larger than life.

He uncorks a swing. The sharp crack of the bat signals another of his legendary home runs – this one far up into the left field bleachers. What is the batter's secret?

It's the same secret of famous basketball player Michael Jordan, and tennis legend Serena Williams. And this secret is not just limited to athletes – it is at the heart of the remarkable success of famous artists, writers, inventors, business leaders, and even chess masters and media celebrities.

What the batter did was to clear his mind and enter a very special state of consciousness known as "the flow." And if you have ever seen a top athlete in action, you noticed they did not stop everything and sit down to meditate. They just effortlessly focused and then did what they had to do.

It is especially interesting to note what happens to the concept of time in the flow. It almost seems as though the usual laws of physics no longer apply – like being in another dimension where everything slips into slow motion. The baseball racing toward the batter at 101 miles an hour seems to drift slowly through space, and becomes an easy target for the batter.

What is this mysterious "flow" that allows some people to step outside the limitations of time? It's right there in your brain! And learning how to create this mental experience has the potential to dramatically improve the quality of your entire life, and lay your goals right in your lap!

A new study by research teams at Yale, Harvard, Massachusetts General Hospital and MIT shows that meditation seems to cause increased cortical thickness. The structural changes occur in areas of the brain important for sensory, cognitive and emotional processing – all areas that are involved in the "flow" experience.

"What is most fascinating to me is the suggestion that meditation practice can change anyone's grey matter," said Jeremy Gray, assistant professor of psychology. "The study participants were people with jobs and families. They just meditated on average 40 minutes each day -- you don't have to be a monk."

What IS the Flow?

Where did the concept of "the flow" come from? In the late 1930s an unusual European young man looked out through the chaos of war and asked some probing questions. He wanted to understand why so many people feel their lives have been wasted? And why their life is spent in anxiety and unhappiness?"

Hungarian Mihalyi Csikszentmihalyi (pronounced "chicks-sent-me-high") resolved to find an answer. He earned a PhD from the University of Chicago, then spent the next twenty-five years interviewing people around the world from all walks of life. He asked each of them to recall the happiest moments of their life, and to describe what created those moments.

He discovered an amazing sameness in their answers. "The best moments," he writes in his book *Flow: The Psychology of Optimal Experience*, "usually occur when a person's body or mind is stretched to its limits in a voluntary, highly focused effort to accomplish something difficult and worthwhile."

"Such experiences are not necessarily pleasant at the time they occur," Csikszentmihalyi explains. "The swimmer's muscles might have ached during his most memorable race, his lungs might have felt like exploding, and he might have been dizzy with fatigue – yet these could have been the best moments of his life."

Flow Builds Mind Power

Csikszentmihalyi describes the experience of "being in the flow" as being completely involved in an activity for its own sake. Your sense of ego falls away. Time stops or seems to fly by. Every action, movement, and thought follows inevitably from the previous one, just like playing jazz. Your whole being is focused and involved, and you use your skills and talents to the utmost.

He determined that a state of flow occurs when we are totally absorbed in an activity that is neither too easy nor too difficult for us. If the activity is too easy, we become bored. If it is too difficult we become anxious or stressed. But if the activity is just right, we can enter into a state of flow just like children at play.

What Csikszentmihalyi stresses is this -- the doorway into the flow is to create absolutely crystal-clear mental focus.

Csikszentmihalyi found that being in the flow actually increases your mind power. Additionally, the longer you remain "in flow," the more complex and highly developed your brain becomes on both physical and mental levels.

Just how does this increase mind power? When you enter into and sustain flow-level focus, you stimulate the creation of new, more complex, brain networks.

This further increases your capability to focus. It also increases your brain's access to both new and old data. In short, being in the flow makes you mentally quicker and smarter. Does this sound like something you'd like to have in your life?

Being in "The Flow"

You often move into and out of lower levels of the flow without realizing it. Any stimulating activity that completely fills your conscious attention can put you there. But the minute you feel worry, boredom or insecurity creeping in, you are immediately kicked out of the flow.

The secret is being mentally focused in the present moment -- fully alert and mentally clear. In short, you must be totally involved in the "now." The minute you let your focus drift into the past or the future, you're out. So, the better your ability to focus your mind, the faster you will achieve flow. What you want to do is to train your brain to totally focus in the present moment.

How to Get Started With "The Flow"

Forget the Past and Future. To enter the Flow it is important to clear your mind and bring it into the present moment.

Ask yourself this: Is there something wrong in this

very moment? Perhaps you have received a "pink slip" and are being laid off from work?

Clear that out of your mind by placing it where it belongs -- the possible future. It has not happened yet. The same goes for anything in the past. Do not recreate the past in the present moment by thinking about it. Just let the past go for now.

Then just totally focus on what is happening at this very moment. You will become aware of just sitting in a comfortable environment reading this. You should find nothing wrong with the present moment. Once focused in the present, ask yourself these questions:

1. Am I waiting for something to happen?
2. To have more time?
3. To make more money?
4. To meet the right person?
5. For the "right" opportunity?

Waiting is a game the mind plays because it doesn't have the discipline to focus in the present moment. Do this for a few minutes every day and track your progress. You will refine your ability to focus in the now.

Be Aware of Your Thoughts. If you find your mind drifting or filled with anxiety, you've moved away from the flow. Refocus on the task at hand, and adjust the difficulty until you become fully engaged in the task itself.

The next time you're driving or walking around, focus closely on what's happening around you. Listen to the sounds, observe the people. Do not focus on what you have to do, what happened yesterday, or what could happen tomorrow. Focus your attention only on what is happening right now.

Surrender to the Process. This is perhaps the greatest mystery of the Flow process. As you practice flow you will find yourself enjoying the process of simply focusing completely on the present task without straining or undue effort.

As this happens you will begin to experience brief periods of timelessness. This is the doorway into the level of flow experienced by world-class athletes when they set personal records, and it is both calm and exhilarating at the same time.

Embrace Ecstasy. The most interesting part of this process is the natural result of the previous steps.

You're going to suddenly be hit from out of nowhere with an overwhelming feeling of ecstasy.

You'll recognize it. When it happens, you are solidly in the Flow. Such a sensation of ecstasy is actually a whole brain event in which your entire cortex shakes like a bowl of jello. This experience is unmistakable. Your productivity will attain unheard of heights – all because you are focused in the present moment.

Dr. Jill Ammon-Wexler

TEN. YOUR QUANTUM LEAP

Bob and Jennifer had always been hard workers. They raised two kids, helped them through college, and were ready to finally retire. They still had a mortgage on their home, but were working with an investment counselor to boost their holdings to cover that.

He's always given them good advice, and they've temporarily moved their savings into futures to take advantage of a big rush on high tech stocks.

On the morning of September 11, 2001 Bob and Jennifer were "camping out" at their little cabin on a lake near Portland – a marriage gift from Bob's parents 38 years ago.

They pulled into the dock just before two o'clock and saw a large group of people gathered on their neighbors' deck. Something didn't feel quite right, so they tied up their boat and walked over to make sure their neighbors were OK.

There was no way they could be prepared for the shock awaiting them.

Their neighbors had placed a portable TV on the picnic table, and it was tuned into CBS news. The shocking images focused on downtown New York, still stunned and shuttering from the impact of the 9-11 attack on the World Trade Center.

Jennifer's first thought was of their son who worked two buildings over from the South Tower. She bolted off the deck and headed for the telephone. It was almost midnight before they reached their son, who proved to be badly shaken, but otherwise fine.

It was well into the next morning before Bob noticed the message waiting light on the telephone was blinking.

He returned the call, then collapsed into a chair as their investment counselor told him the stock market had reacted negatively to the attack, and there had been a series of "calls" against their futures.

The market did not recover. Bob and Jennifer's savings were wiped out in the space of three days. The couple now faced some serious decisions.

Essentially, their entire life savings were gone. They couldn't afford the mortgage on their house, and the only property they owned outright was a very run-down cabin on the lake.

Lesser problems have caused people to actually jump out windows. But Bob and Jennifer had built a resource of mental strength over the years. They looked at what they had left, and decided to take a quantum leap.

What did they do?

They listed their house for a quick sale, pulled out their equity, and invested it to fix the cabin on the lake. It is today a popular and prosperous "bring your own boat" camping and RV center.

The couple today feels this was the most wonderful thing that could have happened to them. Happy? Oh yes, and also totally debt-free.

Rapid Change = True Power

The hard blow that slammed against Bob and Jennifer almost instantly wiped out their somewhat comfortable lifestyle, but it also created the space for a quantum leap into a positive personal change.

Personal catastrophe often automatically leads to the necessity for a dramatic personal change. But are catastrophe and loss necessary to instantly create a dramatically improved personal reality? Or is there another way? And is it true that such changes do not last?

Remember the early *Star Trek* series in which Scotty, the head engineer, was asked to "beam up" his shipmates using the spaceship's teleportation system? In his book *Ageless Body, Timeless Mind*, Dr. Deepak Chopra describes how the nervous system of a snail can help us understand how this concept fits into making a personal quantum leap.

Snails, Chopra explains, have a nervous system that fires very slowly compared to our human nervous systems. A snail therefore requires many seconds to "register" a change in its visual field, while we humans require only a tiny fraction of a second.

Here's how this gets interesting: If you walk rapidly past a snail you won't even be "registered" as having been there, explains Chopra.

And if you drop a penny in front of the snail, the penny will seem to the snail to have "appeared from nowhere." And, Chopra adds, if you pick up a snail and move it quickly, the snail will have a sense it has been "teleported" from one place to another.

Our human senses play a similar trick. There is simply no way we can actually "see" the material world flash in and out of existence thousands of times each second.

Our brains make things appear solid, just like movies are created by connecting a series of still photographs to form a streaming image. So we "see" things as solid, although they are actually flashing in and out of quantum manifestation.

So what then is reality?

If you examine what scientists are now telling us, everything is so uncertain it is actually unpredictable. But as Chopra reminds us, "where there is uncertainty there's a chance for freedom."

As one famous Indian guru once told his followers, reality is like a net. If you want to escape it, find a hole and jump through. The remainder of this chapter contains a plan of action to help you find that hole, then take a quantum leap into an exciting new "personal level of reality."

Prepare For a Quantum Leap

If you have read a few "personal growth" books, you've probably run into the common assumption that empowerment and change require very systematic step-by-step, gradual changes over time.

Is that assumption wrong? No. It does work. Gradual change is achievable and even sensible for many folks. And if you persist and do not surrender to boredom or discouragement, you may eventually create some lasting personal improvements.

However taking a quantum leap provides far more remarkable results, and an entirely new and exciting personal reality. Have you ever done something "impossible" or totally out of the ordinary? Even if it was a small impossibility, what you experienced was a "quantum leap."

This might be as radical as suddenly quitting your job and boarding a plane for a new life in Costa Rica – or as seemingly "small" as suddenly deciding to make up with a friend, and instantly grabbing the phone to call them.

A quantum leap is personal change on an immediate, limitation-dissolving level. It is you literally erasing your old assumptions, achieving amazing mental clarity, and instantly creating a new self with entirely new potentials.

Taking a quantum leap goes beyond the concept of gradual personal changes. It feels more like what Deepak Chopra's imaginary snail would experience if it was picked up and placed in what seems to be a totally different "reality."

Sound impossible?

It's not!

Remember? You have a brain that travels through time from the past out into the future, that creates illusions of solidness out of vibrating energy flashing in and out of physical manifestation, and that has so many "smart cells" they could stretch thousands of miles. You create your own reality with your thoughts. Your so-called limitations are also your creation, and can be "un-created."

You CAN Do It!

Is it realistic to believe that YOU can achieve such a radical leap forward? Let's answer that with a few questions:

1. Do you have a dream you passionately wish to achieve?
2. Are you willing to become the person that dream belongs to?
3. Are you willing to challenge your assumptions and beliefs?
4. Can you tolerate some "uncertainty" if it promises to move you in the desired direction?

If your answers are "yes," you're a great candidate for a personal quantum leap. The remainder of this chapter will lead you through the process. If your answers are "no," you may change your mind when you discover how achievable such a dramatic personal empowerment can be.

Quantum Leaps and Physics

Serious thinker Christopher Westra tells us, "The laws of quantum physics show that everything must be created first in the inner world.

The inner reality is the matrix, the blueprint, or divine design, and then physical matter is attracted to this 'template' by the laws of quantum attraction. This is how the world you see comes into existence!"

The term quantum leap is actually a term from quantum physics. It refers to the capability of a particle to make a jump from one place to another spontaneously, without any apparent effort, and without passing through the space between the particle's starting and ending positions.

This has overwhelming implications when applied to our human existence.

Remember – you are made up of the same stuff as that particle. In his book entitled *Taking the Quantum Leap*, author Fred Alan Wolf says this, "Taking the quantum leap means taking a risk, going off into an uncharted territory with no guide to follow." OK. It's now time for YOU to write a new chapter in the book of your life.

What follows is only a road map. Your feet must walk upon the path, you must select the forks in the road to take, and you must take the leap into "uncharted territory with no guide to follow."

Ready? Do you feel restless and uncertain about what to do? Or perhaps you're facing a "loss" and wondering what comes next? Both of these are actually opportunities for taking a quantum leap.

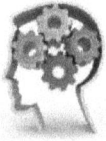

A quantum leap starts with deciding exactly what personal reality you want to land in. Who do you want to become?

You now realize you actually create your own reality with your thoughts.

This takes the "power of manifestation" to an entirely new level. It all starts in your physical brain, and you now have the basic knowledge required to really put that brain to work.

How to Move Forward

Go where it's "Hot." In deciding where you want to land, a big secret is this: Aim for where your energy is hottest.

Ask yourself what makes you feel most alive, and go toward that. Aim for the direction you feel most strongly pulled toward – whether it's business or art, moving to Paris, or starting a little fix-and-sell home remodeling business!

 Once you have a clear vision, the leap awaits you. Just immediately and passionately go for it! You will instantly get a clear vision of your true strength when you direct your life into your true passion.

Remember that success is the process of BECOMING the person your goal belongs to. The power of a quantum leap is that you INSTANTLY commit to BE that person.

Basically this is achieved by making a passionate and irreversible commitment to focus your life on actually achieving your goal. This is true for any goal you passionately desire – whether it's tied to business, personal, relationship, spiritual or social interests.

Contemplate these phrases in the above paragraph:

- Passionate,
- Irreversible commitment,
- Desire,
- Focus your life, and
- Instantly become that person.

Get started by digging into your dream. Really reflect on it deeply. Do you truly have a passion to land in that dream? If not, look into yourself and ask what you really do passionately want to achieve. Look for what you are willing to make a total commitment to.

Forget the Comfortable. Now I am going to suggest something that might at first seem totally crazy. Take a few minutes to think back over what you've done in the past that really seemed to "work" for you. Maybe you have always been a methodical, careful thinker?

Then forget it! Perhaps you've tended to be creative and spontaneous? *Now forget this too.*

Forget every method and strategy you have successfully used in the past. And especially forget the methods and strategies you feel are your "strongest cards." Why? Because if they were truly your "finest," you would already be the person your dream belongs to!

Taking a quantum leap into a new level of personal reality and potential requires abandonment of the old you. The things you did in the past might have worked before, but they can also lock you into using the same approach over and over. And that will simply deliver the same old results.

That old saying, "If at first you don't succeed, try, try again" is not going to take you into an exciting quantum leap. Turning the knob of a locked door will never get you through that door. You need to find another way in, or around, or kick the door in.

I remember when I was learning the sport of power lifting years ago from an amazing coach and her husband. I was cycling up for a competition, and kept "trying harder" with my deadlift.

But it seemed the harder I tried, the less successful I became.

Then during my last practice session before a State competition I tried so hard the bar threw me over backwards. The 224-pound loaded bar landed on my chest, pinning me to the platform. It took two men to lift the bar off my prone body.

Now you can bet that was a humbling moment of truth about the wisdom of trying harder.

But an interesting thing happened. When it came time for the competition six days later, I had been cured of "trying harder" in the deadlift. When my name was called I stepped onto the platform, twisted my hands into the sharply knurled bar, and just totally forgot about "proper form."

I saw the judge's signal, and dropped down into the lift.

Suddenly I found myself surrounded by a thick white fog. I could hear the shouts of the crowd, but they seemed to come from miles away. The heavily stacked barbell felt weightless. I rose easily into the top of the lift, saw the green light, and returned the

276-pound weight to the floor like a feather.

My coach was stunned. "You could have lifted another 50 pounds," she gasped.

She was right. I had taken a quantum leap into a personal capacity far beyond "trying harder." How did I do this? By releasing everything I had been trying over and over, then just "allowing" a higher personal wisdom to step into place.

YOU *have that same capacity!*

Get Radical. What can you do to tap into your own personal wisdom and power? Start by becoming absolutely determined to allow yourself to commit to some new, unproven behaviors and strategies. In short—to catapult yourself right out of the comfort zone of what has "always worked."

The comfort zone is deadly to anyone with a passionate dream. Doing the same old thing over and over just gives you more of the same results.

To take a quantum leap you have got to break the chains of the familiar and embrace the "impossible."

What does the "impossible" look like? Actually more times than not you might have assumed it is "too simple." It may be just rolling up your pant legs and wading across a stream rather than cutting two trees to fall across the water, then spending hours building a bridge. But at the time it seemed impossible because you assumed the current was too swift, making the "easy" solution impossible.

Brilliant solutions to achieving your dream are often barely concealed as the simplest possible solution. It may in fact be so simple you would normally not even recognize it as a solution. That is why it's so important to commit to trying the "too simple, crazy approaches" we often discover almost accidentally.

Just let go of your comfortable old assumptions, forget being logical, and open yourself to "impossible" elegantly simple solutions that will let you soar through life and take one quantum leap after another.

Focus on What You Want. Remember how your emotional brain works to manifest what you focus on? This is why you want to focus on what you want -- on where you want to land. Forget any road blocks or problems you think might stand in your way. If you focus on problems, you will strengthen their hold on you.

Making a quantum leap to your dream requires moving far beyond what you think is "possible." It is important to focus your mental sights on your desired end result. Do not worry about how you'll get there. Remember? A quantum leap is an effortless leap from one point to another – without covering the space in between.

Allow yourself to daydream, to risk so-called failure, and to embrace and expect the "impossible." Remember, you're NOT looking for a gradual, step-by-step improvement in your performance and capabilities. You are going after landing in an entirely new reality, just like Deepak Chopra's tiny snail.

Just Believe. Your brain is the most dynamic, changeable organ of your body. Scientists have proven our brains constantly change to adapt to our circumstances. We now know that each choice we make, each new thing we learn, instantly creates physical changes in our brain.

At this very moment, as you read these words, your brain is changing on a very real physical level. Brand new brain cell-to-cell connections are being created, and old connections are being modified or eliminated.

 The power of your thoughts is beyond concept. You literally DO become what you think about. This is no longer just a "saying" -- it's now an accepted, scientifically-proven fact!

Take a moment to look around you with open eyes. Unless you have visual challenges, you can see the furniture around you, the walls of the room, the view out the windows, other people who are present, etc. When you close your eyes, on the other hand, inner images and thoughts unrelated to the physical reality come to your attention. Your imagination takes you beyond the limits of space and time as you preview future possibilities.

There's now solid scientific proof that we each actually create our own reality with our thoughts. **Researchers around the world agree that our thoughts actually cause things to happen in the physical world.**

We now know from quantum physics, for example, that subatomic particles will physically manifest IF there is someone there to observe them. So build passionate desire and belief in your vision, and trust life to bring it right to you.

Forget "Ordinary" Reality. Your mental vision of what is "real" for you is far more powerful than the "reality" happening around you. Remember? This is the direct result of how your subconscious mind works. As I shared earlier, your subconscious mind is NOT analytical. It simply accepts what is presented to it as real.

Suppose you have a dream of becoming a millionaire business person or a great artist. You can use the process of active mental visualization to create a clear and detail "future memory" of how that quantum landing spot looks -- and then transport yourself there.

Act As If. Remember the power of "acting as if" you are already the person to whom your dream belongs? "Acting as if" works. As you repeat your "acting," you are building very real physical brain networks dedicated to the person you are "acting like." This builds stronger and stronger networks in your brain, and your acting will soon gain the physical brain strength of a belief. And as you already know, "Whatever you believe will become your reality."

Do you have a dream of doing something outrageous in your life? If you have the desire, it will become a reality if you begin to passionately "act it out." Put your heart and all your passion into it!

Embrace Uncertainty. There's simply no way you can control everything happening "out in the world." But you CAN control how you respond. The larger your quantum leap, the more chaos you may at first experience.

This is not bad! Radical change shakes up all of your old familiar beliefs and assumptions. The more willing you are to face some temporary chaos and call it a creative opportunity, the more successful your leap will be. Allow yourself to feel a little bit of discomfort as you land in your new shoes!

Expect the Unexpected. Suddenly leaping into the shoes of the person to whom your dream belongs takes you beyond anything you might expect. So, expect the unexpected. Expect people to see and respond to you differently. Expect "accidental" circumstances to pop up, and invite them into your life. Especially listen to your intuition, and act on it. Above all else, trust and rely on the force of your desire and beliefs to bring the components of your dream to you in all manner of unexpected events, people, and opportunities.

Life Begins When YOU Do

Tucked in between the moments of our lives are phrases like: "When things slow down, or when I finish my degree, or when the kids are grown, or when I get well, or when I get a new job, or when whatever happens –THEN I will follow my dream."

 That dream in your heart is there because it most likely already IS you. You just need to give it a chance to bloom.

If you dream it, BEGIN it.

If you have an idea, EMBRACE it.

If there is longing, ACKNOWLEDGE it.

If there is mission, COMMIT to it.

The life you want begins the <u>instant</u> you commit to QUANTUM LEAP INTO IT!

ELEVEN. OUR OTHER OFFERINGS...

 **YOUR NEXT STEP?**

Break Free is a great choice to set your feet on the path to increased personal empowerment. Available as a Kindle, an audio book, or a printed book -- as are many of our books! Click the link for a FREE PREVIEW=> **http://www.BuildMindPower.com**

 **LIKE TO EXPLORE?**

Come visit our website to explore our audio books, ebooks, printed books, brainwave training collections, special training programs AND our collection of great articles=> **http://www.BuildMindPower.com**

BRAIN TRAINING AUDIOS

The author of this book, Dr. Jill Ammon-Wexler, is a world renowned pioneer of brain/mind and consciousness research. Come explore her UNIQUE collection of engineered brainwave trainings to help you rapidly experience positive effects. Check it out here=> **http://QuantumLeapAudios.com/**

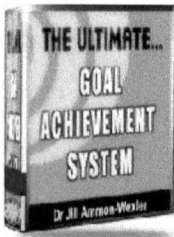

The ULTIMATE GOAL SYSTEM

Overcome the #1 reason most people never reach their goals. An evening with this 62-page training and integrated workbook will power-up your life (or your business) in some very surprising and positive ways. A complete GOAL ACHIEVEMENT SYSTEM=> **http://www.quantum-self.com/goals.htm**

Build a QUANTUM MIND!

Are YOU one of those special people with a burning desire to achieve more in your life? If so ... Dr. Ammon-Wexler personally invites **YOU** to come participate in her unique QUANTUM MIND training program.

Develop and refine your brain and mind power in the comfort of your own home. This exciting 3-month training program is packed with unique training audios, videos and specially engineered brainwave training.

Your end results include: Greatly increased creativity, clear mental focus, refined intelligence, instant stress management, mental clarity, and superior levels of brain/mind performance.

Go learn more, and take advantage of a <u>deep book buyer's discount</u>=>**<u>http://www.HotBrainz.com</u>**

Dr. Jill Ammon-Wexler

MEET THE AUTHOR

Jill Ammon-Wexler is a doctor of positive psychology, pioneer brain/mind researcher, a committed life adventurer, and the author of over 30 books, hundreds of articles and research reports, and numerous popular personal empowerment training programs.

She founded California's Human Dynamics Workshop and the InnerSpace Center, where she conducted Esalen-inspired intensive workshops and mind power training. She also served as an advisor to President Jimmy Carter's Special Presidential Commission on Women in Business.

Her mentors have included: Angeles Arien, Gia Fu-Feng, Soygal Rinpoche, Sri Anandi Ma, Abraham Maslow, Jay McCullough, Jacob Moreno, Virginia Satir, Bruce Ogilvie, Fritz Perls, Alan Watts and many other higher states of consciousness experts.

Her other passions include home design and remodeling, gardening, being out of doors, skiing, art painting, and making a positive difference in the lives of her readers and students.

Dr. Jill Ammon-Wexler

www.ingramcontent.com/pod-product-compliance
Lightning Source LLC
Chambersburg PA
CBHW070958040426
42443CB00007B/567